The Ministry of Helps Handbook

How To Be Totally Effective Serving in the Ministry of Helps

by
Buddy Bell

Harrison House
Tulsa, Oklahoma

Unless otherwise indicated, all Scripture quotations are taken from the *King James Version* of the Bible.

14th Printing

The Ministry of Helps Handbook —
How To Be Totally Effective
Serving in the Ministry of Helps
ISBN 0-89274-766-8
Copyright © 1990 by Buddy Bell
P. O. Box 27366
Tulsa, Oklahoma 74149

Published by Harrison House, Inc.
P. O. Box 35035
Tulsa, Oklahoma 74153

Contents

Foreword

Buddy Bell operates a unique gift of God for the Body of Christ in establishing the ministry of helps.

His many years of practical experience in two of America's outstanding local churches qualify him as an expert in this vital area of ministry. He brings a sense of dignity to the jobs that for many years have been slighted by wrong thinking, and he stirs workers in churches and ministries to new heights of service for the Lord.

The impact of his ministry on our church workers revolutionized our ministry. I heartily recommend the teachings of Buddy Bell on audio cassette, video tape, or in person!

Willie George
Pastor, Church On The Move
Tulsa, Oklahoma

* * *

"People *called* to pass buckets, change diapers, take care of children? I've got to see about this!"

Yes, those were a few of my thoughts as I entered into the workshop on "Helps in the Local Church," held by the Rev. Buddy Bell. To my astonishment, Rev. Bell began to unveil scripture after scripture, teaching on this wonderful, much-misunderstood, but greatly needed ministry.

At times, I would cry, and at other times, laugh, as Brother Bell corrected my improper thinking. Yet he still inspired me to roll up my sleeves and get busy with the work of the ministry.

As you read this book, I trust that you, too, will be inspired to enter into this vast, virtually untapped work of "the Ministry of Helps."

J. Phillip Tasker, Pastor
Door of Faith Christian Center
Dunedin, Florida

* * *

This complete book on the Ministry of Helps is a joy to read. This book is an excellent definer and equipper concerning the almost unknown realm of helps. Not only is it stimulating reading, but also challenging and informative.

I know this book is going to be used mightily of God in the Church today. The days of only a small percentage of the Body of Christ doing a hundred percent of the work of God are over. I believe this book will greatly help the Church.

I am going to use this book for my entry-level workers in particular, as well as a refresher for those already in the process of serving.

I thank God that Buddy Bell has allowed himself to be used by God in his particular call. Our church would not have been able to do all the things we have done without God having used Rev. Bell to teach us in the area of helps.

Stephen Johnson, Pastor
His Church Christian Fellowship
Escondido, California

Preface

A lot of people ask how I have learned so much about the ministry of helps. How did I get started — did I have a degree in speech or management? I have even been accused of having a degree in acting!

The truth is that only the Lord knows what I have gone through to get to this point. Anything I have been able to do or to teach has come through divine revelation and hard experience in walking that revelation out in everyday operations of churches and ministries.

I have been rejected, spit on, shoved around, and humiliated. But I had no doubt all of the time that I was where God wanted me to be. Basically, I am a farmer with a high school education. Then I worked in a factory for more than six years before becoming born again.

As a baby Christian, I was so "fired up" that people told me Jesus wanted me in the ministry. I ran off to a Bible school and found out at that time that I was *not* called to pulpit ministry. The pastor of the first church in which my wife and I were involved understood the ministry of helps. He opened a door for me to serve in the church. That pastor did not look at my credentials, but at my attitude.

He said, "If there are two people, one with no ability but an attitude of faithfulness, and the other with a lot of ability but no faithfulness, I will take the one who is faithful everytime."

In Bible school, I was my pastor's "handyman" for a while, and I did everything I was asked to do. And the Lord was careful to warn me not to become too familiar with my "boss."

He said to me very strongly, "Buddy, you are not part of this family."

So whenever the family were gathered together in one room, I would go to another room. If I became intimate and too familiar, I would have lost the perspective on what God wanted me to do in the ministry. The pastor paid me, but I would have worked for free because the Lord had laid it on my heart.

Anyone who is working primarily for money is working for man and not for Jesus. If you serve Jesus, He will reward you and take care of you, and it will not affect your attitude. I believe Christian workers should be paid as well as possible. However, if they will not do as good a job for Jesus and for free — if necessary — then we need to look at their intent for service.

I learned from the leadership that God has set me under during the years that I worked actively in the ministry of helps. People never go beyond leadership. Whatever leadership does, that is what the people are willing to do. As a pastor or church leader, if you want faithful and committed workers, be faithful and committed.

If you want to reap a crop, you have to plant some seed. You have to stay out in front of your people; then, they will step up to where you were. Apple trees beget apples. Pastors do not beget sheep. Sheep beget sheep. Nursery workers beget nursery workers. Ushers beget ushers. Every Christian has a responsibility to reproduce himself or herself.

Reproduce in someone else what God has placed in you. Get someone else excited about the job you are doing. Then, as they replace you, you will be amazed at what God has next for you.

Churches need the helps ministry operating now more than ever, I believe. When you turn on television today, what office do you see represented most often? Pastors. More pastors are taking the lead in the Church than since the early days of this century.

I believe this next (perhaps the last in these endtimes) move of God is coming through the local church. We need to get back to the Word of God and let pastors function the way they are supposed to. Pastors are a gift from God and spokesmen for Jesus. They need to be free to operate as gifts and spokesmen for the Lord.

Every Christian can do something to help with the natural running of the church, in order to free the pastor to concentrate on the spiritual things. But workers have to have the zeal to be faithful and obedient to those set over them.

I pray that this book will change not only your Christian walk but your local church.

A pastor's friend,
Rev. Buddy Bell

Part One:
Faithfulness
Is the Crowbar of God

1

The Anointing of the Ministry of Helps

Several years ago, I was holding a Ministry of Helps Seminar in a church in Midland, Michigan. The temperature was forty degrees below zero, and the three major highways into that area all were closed because of snow.

Nevertheless, our services were continuing. Before one of the meetings, I began to have a "discussion" with the Lord over what He wanted me to teach that night — which I did not want to teach!

Have you ever argued with God when He asked you to do something? We would all make it easier on ourselves just to be obedient in the beginning, because of course, He knows what He is doing, and we do not. But I was pacing back and forth in my motel room telling the Lord I did not want to teach on this subject (which He already knew)!

The Lord had been after me for months to teach a certain thing, and in addition, my wife was urging me to obey the Lord.

Knowing the Lord was urging me, she would say, "Buddy, you've got to teach it," and I would answer, "Honey, I really don't want to teach that sort of thing."

So there I was, alone in a motel room, snowed in, and once again arguing with God. As we tend to do, I thought if I explained it to God, He would surely begin to see my side of the situation — as if He did not know the situation already.

"People give me weird looks when I even mention it, Lord. They act strange, or they act as if I am strange. I just don't want to do it, Lord."

In my mind, I could hear my wife's voice again as I struggled with the Lord: "Buddy, you've got to do it."

Then the Lord said clearly, "I want you to do it tonight."

The subject He wanted me to teach was "the anointing for the ministry of helps."

My objection was that people want to hear about supernatural manifestations — signs, wonders, miracles, and special anointings — but, most of the time, they do not want to hear about doing the work of God in a serving capacity.

Another thing that bothered me was that people often came up to me and said, "Buddy, *you* really have an anointing for the ministry of helps. You really do!"

They acted as if I were the only one who had that anointing. I began to think that perhaps there *was* no anointing for the ministry of helps. Perhaps God had just felt He had to give me something extra to help me out.

Often, I had reasoned with the Lord, saying, "I just can't believe there is an 'anointing for the ministry of helps,' at least not for the whole Body of Christ. I don't want to teach it, Lord. I just don't want to do it."

That night, the Lord would tell me to teach on the anointing, and I would refuse. Just when it seemed neither of us would budge, something unusual happened. This event changed my entire outlook concerning my teaching on the ministry of helps.

What I am going to share is *the absolute truth*. I feel the necessity to make that statement, just as Jesus used to say *verily* before some of the things He said. That word *verily* was a witness that what He was about to say was *the absolute truth*, not a parable.

Also, I can remember sitting in a congregation listening to a man of God tell about a supernatural experience and thinking, "Boy, has he got an imagination!"

So, in case you are tempted to think that about the following event, I want you to know that it really happened.

A Pool of Anointing

Suddenly, I felt myself being lifted up and taken out of that motel room. Physically, my body was still in the room, but my spirit being — the real me — was lifted up and taken somewhere else.

I began to feel as if I were floating in water. If you are a swimmer, do you remember how you automatically move your arms when you first get into the water? That is what I began to do, then I began to swim. I felt very strange to be swimming and, yet, standing in a motel room at the same time. But there I was, in both places at once.

Then something else happened: I began to see myself at my home church operating in the ministry of helps, and it was like watching a movie. I saw all the joy, happiness, and strength that was in my life as I ministered. I saw myself during one ten-day period — that actually had happened — as an auditorium was built at my church.

My pastor had gone to Hawaii just before this time period I was seeing in the Lord's "movie."

As he left to board the plane, he had looked at me and said, "I want the church auditorium done in ten days."

Several different kinds of construction engineers told me it could not be done. I figured they knew their jobs, and I had never handled a project that big before. But the pastor said he wanted it done in ten days, and that was my order — so it had to be done in ten days.

The auditorium would seat three thousand people and had a 35-foot-long, 16-foot-wide platform with seven steps leading up to it. That was only the main platform. There were to be two smaller platforms on either end of the main one. The pastor wanted all of the platform area carpeted in bright red.

The engineers said, "There is no way to get that much carpet in ten days, Buddy. A mill takes that long to make it, then it has to be finished and shipped and so forth."

(Later, we learned the local carpet mill had shut down for lack of work, so when we called with our large order, they got it out in three days!)

However, as I watched Buddy Bell in the supernatural "movie," I heard several different people tell me that the job could not be done. I saw a living panorama as that ten days played out in detail, and I can tell you, my mind was going absolutely *wild* as I watched.

Every now and then, I would hear myself reply to some of those objections, "Well, the pastor said he wants it done in ten days, and it will be done in ten days."

In the midst of this challenge with all of its tests and trials, I again saw the joy, happiness, and strength I had experienced during that construction project. We would work 16 to 18 hours at a stretch, go home and rest for two hours, and come right back to work. I saw how refreshed I was after very little sleep, as if I had slept like a baby through an entire night.

Then suddenly, all of the joy and strength I had just been observing in the "movie" of myself was magnified a hundred times as I "swam" in that wonderful water.

"Oh, boy, this is *nice*," I said.

I was experiencing strength as I had never known it before. I felt as if I could push a wall in with my bare hands. There was joy within me such as I had never experienced. The happiness, joy, and strength of being in the ministry of helps filled me up supernaturally and surrounded me. I kept saying, "Boy, this is nice," over and over.

"Oh, Lord," I cried, "Where am I now?"

He said, "You are in the pool of the 'anointing for the ministry of helps' that has been lying dormant in heaven for thousands and thousands of years."

He lifted me gently out of the pool as quickly as He had put me in it and took me off in the distance for a "bird's-eye" view. And I saw a tremendous pool of water as clear as glass, with a very large crack in the bottom where the anointing was dripping out.

"Buddy," the Lord said, "there have been very few people who have gotten under those drips and stayed there. They became afraid and removed themselves from under the anointing.

Perhaps 99 percent of the Christians in any given church have experienced the anointing for the ministry of helps, but it frightened them, and they ran away. Let me give you an example.

Your pastor may get up on a Sunday morning and say, "We need someone to come in next week and sweep the auditorium."

Your hand goes up, then you think it over a bit, and quickly pull it down. Why?

You pulled down your hand because a thought such as, "What's wrong with me? I don't have that kind of time," came into your mind. At that moment, you experienced the anointing of the ministry of helps. But you listened to the "second thought" and literally removed yourself from under those drips.

I will tell you where you got the idea to volunteer. You were under the anointing of the ministry of helps for a moment. The anointing gives you joy, happiness, strength.

understanding, and even the ability to carry out the plans of God for your church.

At the time you volunteer, you experience the anointing, and it causes great faith to arise within. You feel as if you can do anything the pastor wants you to do. The roots of strength, joy, and happiness are beginning to grow deep.

If you back up, you are refusing the anointing. That stops a move of God in your life, and a job God had prepared for you will go undone.

A Challenge From God

The next thing the Lord said to me was something I really liked: "Buddy, I want to challenge you. I want you to crack open the pool of anointing and spread it out all over the Body of Christ, because My people need it."

"How am I ever going to do that?" I asked.

He said, "I gave you a 'crowbar' more than three and a half years ago. I want you to take that crowbar and crack open the pool of the anointing for the ministry of helps."

After the Lord said that, I stood there for a moment with a blank expression on my face that reflected a blank mind.

I thought, "*Crowbar? Crowbar?* Here I am having this great spiritual experience with the Lord, and He says 'crowbar.' Couldn't He give me some nice Hebrew or Greek word? Or something more spiritual sounding than crowbar?"

I grew up on a farm, and I knew all about crowbars. Every farmer that I ever knew had one particular crowbar that he liked to use. On our farm, we had one that you apparently could use for about anything.

Our corn dump was stuck once, and I yelled, "Hey, Grandpa! The corn dump's stuck!"

He yelled back, "Well, get the crowbar."

So I would run and get that old crowbar, knowing it would get the job done. There were times when I would think that crowbar would snap in two, but I would pry with it until whatever was jammed came unjammed. Our crowbar could do anything — even pull up rocks many times its own weight.

The Lord was speaking my language when he said "crowbar," but I did not know what that represented. What had God given me that was supposed to be His crowbar? Finally, I had to just ask Him, and He began to explain.

Although I had experienced such a wonderful spiritual revelation, I still did not want to teach about the anointing for the ministry of helps.

I said, "Lord, okay, I know what You are saying. But I don't want to teach about myself. I don't want to teach about Buddy Bell."

He said, "That is all right. You don't have to teach about yourself. There is someone in the Bible who had a crowbar like yours."

"Oh, yeah?" I asked. "Who?

"Elisha," He replied.

Why do we get so excited when Elisha is mentioned? Could it be we get so excited about the supernatural things that happened in his ministry because we think life was all "peaches and cream" for him? Do we think it was some kind of "easy street" for him to follow Elijah, the mighty man of God?

We need to go to the Bible and look at the lives of Elijah and Elisha to understand the "crowbar" that Elisha used. Such "crowbars," as spoken of in these scripture texts, are "personal" in nature, and they are there for you to grab. Begin to use your crowbar as soon as you find it. The crowbar will keep you under the anointing for the ministry of helps. You will be blessed, and the Word of the Lord will begin to be accomplished.

2

Elijah, the Man of God

Before we can understand Elisha and the "crowbar of God," we will have to get a good look at the man he followed — Elijah. He is first mentioned in 1 Kings, chapter 17.

Elijah, the Tishbite, the prophet of God, appeared on the scene with the declaration that there would be no more rain, not even dew on the ground, until he said so. That is exactly what happened.

As you read the story of Elijah, you will find that, during the ensuing drought, he remained for a time by the brook of Cherith. There ravens brought him meat and bread each morning and evening until the brook dried up.

Later, Elijah was sent by God to a widow's house in a town in Zidon, totally out of Israelite territory. He told the widow that if she gave him the last of her food, she would not run out of food again. She obeyed, and the prophet's words came true. When her only son died, Elijah raised him from the dead. Are you beginning to see what sort of man Elisha followed?

About three years later, Elijah challenged the prophets of Baal to prove whose god was God. (1 Kings 18.) The god who consumed the sacrifice by fire would be acknowledged to be the true God, and all would follow Him.

Before he challenged the prophets of Baal, he challenged the people. Men of God always challenge the people of God before they deal with things of Satan or with the world. Elijah said:

> And Elijah came unto all the people, and said, How long halt ye between two opinions? if the Lord be God, follow him: but if Baal, then follow him. And the people answered him not a word.
>
> **1 Kings 18:21**

You cannot get any plainer than that. The people did not answer Elijah. They did not say a word — until after they saw signs and wonders. When they did not answer, Elijah pointed out that he was the only prophet remaining of the true God (a little later, however, the Lord told him there actually were 7,000 people in Israel who had not bowed their knees to Baal). But at the time, Elijah really believed he was the only one left. He was ready to stand against 450 false prophets, because he knew whose God was real.

Showdown at High Noon

The 450 prophets of Baal built their altar, placed their sacrifice on it, and began to cry out to their gods. They cried out and cried out. They cut themselves with knives to draw blood for their gods. But no matter how much time Elijah gave them, no fire came down from heaven to consume the sacrifice.

At noon, the Bible says, Elijah began to mock them.

"What's the matter, guys? Is he asleep? Perhaps he has gone on vacation. Yell a little louder, guys!"

I would not have been surprised if old Elijah was rolling on the ground laughing. Would you be too nervous to mock the prophets of Baal? It is all right to laugh at the devil, but you don't want to laugh at him too much, right? There is no telling what he might do. No, Elijah knew the Lord whom he served.

After the prophets of Baal did all they could to bring down fire, Elijah took over. He rebuilt the altar, placed his sacrifice on it, then called for four barrels of water.

I can see those prophets of Baal asking, "Four barrels of water? Doesn't he know we're in the middle of a drought? Elijah! What are you going to do with all that water?"

"Pour them on the sacrifice."

"Oh, yeah? Listen, we'll get the water for you."

He had those four barrels poured over the sacrifice, then turned around and asked for four more barrels. Those four were poured on, and he asked for four more. So much water poured over that sacrifice that it was soaking wet, and the trench he had dug around the altar was full of water.

Then Elijah prayed a simple prayer:

> And it came to pass at the time of the offering of the evening sacrifice, that Elijah the prophet came near, and said, Lord God of Abraham, Isaac, and of Israel, let it be known this day that thou art God in Israel, and that I am thy servant, and that I have done all these things at thy word.
>
> Hear me, O Lord, hear me, that this people may know that thou art the Lord God, and that thou hast turned their heart back again.
>
> 1 Kings 18:36,37

How interesting that Elijah said **let it be known . . . that I am thy servant.**

Why did he not say, "Let it be known that I am thy prophet? Do this, Lord, because I am your prophet, a mighty man of God."

Even Elijah, who *was* a mighty man of God, understood that God does not move on account of one's status, but on behalf of one's service. You cannot impress God with titles. What impresses Him are His servants. Do you need fire from heaven? Then cry out for it as a servant of God and know with all your heart that He will open the heavens and bring you the miracle you need.

> Then the fire of the Lord fell, and consumed the burnt sacrifice, and the wood, and the stones, and the dust, and licked up the water that was in the trench.
>
> 1 Kings 18:38

God heard his prayer of servanthood!

Afterwards, Elijah told the people to grab all of the prophets of Baal and take them down to the River Jordan, where they were all killed. This incident shows a man of God in action and shows the influence of a man of God. This is the man Elisha is going to follow. We need this background on Elijah to understand Elisha and the crowbar of God.

Elijah was still human. As amazing as all of those things are, something happened that showed the human nature in the prophet of God. As soon as Jezebel, queen of Israel and high priestess, heard that her prophets had been killed, she sent a messenger to Elijah telling him that she was going to have him killed. What did Elijah do? The man who had just called down fire from heaven ran for his life!

We all know what happened after that, right? God gave up on Elijah because he missed it, right? No! When a man of God does miracles before our eyes and then makes one mistake, why do we want to forget him?

God did not forget Elijah, did He? The Bible says God sought out Elijah, found him, and gave him some more assignments. Also, it was at this time that He assigned him a servant, someone to help him.

Who Is the Greatest?

How can anyone think the Church can get along without the ministry of helps, without those who wait on tables, take care of the nursery, or maintain the grounds? The Bible clearly shows us that Jesus considered Himself a servant of the Father. That means that even those in the ministry really are servants. They are simply serving at a different level of authority.

Jesus dealt with this subject when the disciples reached the place where they were arguing about rank among themselves.

Then came to him the mother of Zebedee's children with her sons, worshipping him, and desiring a certain thing of him.

And he said unto her, What wilt thou? She saith unto him, Grant that these my two sons may sit, the one on thy right hand, and the other on the left, in thy kingdom. ("Give my sons status, Lord.")

But Jesus answered and said, Ye know not what ye ask, Are ye able to drink of the cup that I shall drink of, and to be baptized with the baptism that I am baptized with? They say unto him, We are able. ("As long as we get our status." Pride and not humility was operating.)

And he saith unto them, Ye shall drink indeed of my cup and be baptized with the baptism that I am baptized with: but to sit on my right hand, and on my left, is not mine to give, but it shall be given to them for whom it is prepared of my Father.

And when the ten heard it, they were moved with indignation against the two brethren.

But Jesus called them unto him, and said, Ye know that the princes of the Gentiles exercise dominion over them, and they that are great exercise authority upon them.

But it shall not be so among you: but whosoever will be great among you, let him be your minister;

And whosoever will be chief among you, let him be your servant:

Even as the Son of man came not to be ministered unto, but to minister, and to give his life a ransom for many.

Matthew 20:20-28

Jesus said He did not come to earth to be ministered to, but to minister and to give His life as a ransom. We need to go forth and serve.

Would you take care of a dirty house and change the dirty diapers for the children of a family of sinners so they could hear the Word of God?

Would you take food and clothing to a family that does not yet know Jesus?

Would you put someone else first and yourself second?

27

Lift up your head and cry out to God, because our God does not move on behalf of those with status in this world, but on behalf of His servants, those with humble hearts.

3

Elisha, the Servant of the Man of God

Shortly after the episode with the prophets of Baal, when rain was restored to Israel, Elijah found his servant. And the man called to serve also was the man God had chosen to take Elijah's place — Elisha, son of Shaphat. (1 Kings 19:16.) When Elijah saw him, Elisha was plowing with twelve yoke of oxen. (v. 19.)

Notice that Elisha was not a poor man, or he would not have been plowing with that many oxen. When Elijah passed by him, he threw his mantle on Elisha. And Elisha left the oxen and ran after Elijah. Why did he do that?

I believe something powerful happened when the mantle fell on Elisha. I believe that mantle was the anointing, and in the anointing was a lot of love. When the anointing dropped on him, he walked away from everything he had. Something must have happened that moved Elisha very deeply.

The only thing he asked was to have time to go kiss his father and mother goodbye. But Elijah answered with a statement that, at first reading, is puzzling. When you look at the circumstances, Elijah's remark sounds very strange:

> Go back again: for what have I done to thee?
>
> 1 Kings 19:20

Why did Elijah say that? What he was saying, in modern language was: "All right, Elisha. If you are going to follow

29

me, it will have to be between you and God. I'm not going to have anything to do with it!"

Elijah was simply obeying God and making Elisha responsible for his own decision.

We think it would be easier to follow a man of God, who would say, "Hey, the Lord told me I would find you out here! He told me to throw my mantle of anointing over you, because you are going to carry on as a prophet after me."

Instead, Elijah said, "Go on about your business. I have done nothing to cause you to follow me. This is between you and God."

That was the strong point offered to Elisha, the "crowbar." God offered it to him, and he took it.

> **And he** (Elisha) **returned back from him** (Elijah)**, and took a yoke of oxen, and slew them, and boiled their flesh with the instruments of the oxen, and gave unto the people, and they did eat. Then he arose, and went after Elijah, and** (take note of this phrase) *ministered unto him.*
>
> **1 Kings 19:21**

If you study the meaning of *minister* in several different translations of the Bible, you will see that Elisha "served" and "helped" the man of God. The word *minister* means "to contribute to, to serve, to attend, and to wait upon."[1]

Elisha made his own decision. He made it while standing in the middle of a plowed field. There were no bright lights, no sweet sounds of orchestral music, no congregation present to see history being made. There was just the Lord and Elisha, for the man of God had walked on by himself.

You make decisions every day. We all do. What about this one:

---

[1] James Strong, *The Exhaustive Concordance of the Bible* (Nashville: Abingdon, 1890) Hebrew and Chaldee Dictionary, #8334.

"When I walked into this church, I just felt the love of God engulf me. I feel so blessed. I love this place. I'll tell you, this is where God wants me!"

Then two weeks later, you are nowhere to be found in that church. All of us have heard people say these kinds of things. Perhaps you have said them. Elisha's decision was not like that. He made what we call a "quality" decision, one that is settled once and for all, one that brought about a permanent change in his life.

Developing a Crowbar

Elisha followed Elijah and began a lengthy term of service for the man of God. He traveled with him, looked after his clothes, cooked his meals, and did anything else necessary to free the man of God for ministry and for spiritual things.

The only reason Elisha was able to do this was because of that irrevocable decision he made in the field with the oxen. During all those years, he still was not told why he was to follow Elijah. Certainly he was tired at times, hot, sweaty, and dirty. Yet, despite any hardships, he stuck with the words he had spoken many years before.

Some Christians cannot stick with their decisions for two weeks. Then we wonder why people around us want nothing to do with our God. Instead of reflecting Jesus to the world, many of us reflect a God Who looks mixed up, confused, and misguided. Who wants to serve a God like that? But we are quick to run to tell our unsaved friends when God speaks to us.

"But, Buddy," you may say, "Elisha was going to take Elijah's place."

We know that, but Elisha did not.

In all of the incidents related in the Bible about Elijah after this time, Elisha may not be mentioned, but he was there. The servant goes where the master goes. He saw all of the things God did through His man, Elijah.

In Second Kings 1:1,2, the Word says:

> Then Moab rebelled against Israel after the death of Ahab.
>
> And Ahaziah fell down through a lattice in his upper chamber that was in Samaria, and was sick: and he sent messengers, and said unto them, Go, inquire of Baalzebub the god of Ekron whether I shall recover of this disease.

Ahaziah was the king of Israel. Yet here he was sending messengers to ask questions of a pagan god, setting an example of idolatry for the nation.

About that time, the Lord sent an angel to Elijah with some instructions. The Lord told Elijah to intercept the messengers from the king's house in Samaria, the capital of Israel, and speak certain words to them.

In today's language, this is what Elijah said:

"Are you going to the so-called god in Ekron to help you because you think there is no God in Israel? Tell King Ahaziah that because he looked for help from a strange god that he surely will die." (vv. 3,4.)

So the messengers returned to Ahaziah with Elijah's words, and he asked them what the man looked like who had given them this message.

They said, "He was a hairy man with a girdle of leather about his loins." (v. 8.)

The king knew who that was all right: **It is Elijah the Tishbite** (v. 8b).

Ahaziah sent a captain with 50 troops to capture Elijah. They found him sitting on a hill, and the captain shouted to him to come down, because the king wanted him. But Elijah asked God to vindicate His words.

> And Elijah answered and said to the captain of fifty, If I be a man of God, then let fire come down from heaven,

**and consume thee and thy fifty. And there came down fire
from heaven, and consumed him and his fifty.**

2 Kings 1:10

Whoosh! All 51 men were gone. You need to understand
that this is not a fairy tale. This really happened. This fire
is the same kind of fire that burns up houses. This is the
real thing. Elijah called that fire down, and all fifty men plus
the captain were consumed to ashes on the spot.

A Servant Follows His Master

The Bible does not mention Elisha during this incident.
But how can you serve someone if you are not where he
is? Elisha was nearby because he was the servant of the man
of God. Because Elisha was human, I wonder if the thought
entered his mind, like it would enter our minds, to hope
Elijah never got mad at him?

Imagine if a modern pastor suddenly stopped one
Sunday morning in the pulpit and said, "If I be a man of
God, let fire come down out of heaven and consume that
piano." Then whoosh! The piano suddenly burns up, and
nothing around it is touched. The doors of the church would
be torn off by people trying to get out!

I do not believe Elijah had a smile on his face during
this demonstration of God's power. He probably looked
mean enough to chew nails.

If your pastor stood up in church with that look on his
face, what would you do?

Most people would say, "This is the last Sunday I'm
coming here! I'm going to some church where people preach
love and show me some love."

But did you not say *God* told you to attend this church?
Did you not say you *knew* this was where you were supposed
to be?

"Yes, but I didn't know fire was going to be called down
from heaven by the pastor!"

Human nature being the same in Bible days as today, Elisha may have had some questioning thoughts. He may even have considered finding another prophet to serve. But after some reflecting, he soon came back to the scene in the field where he was first called and to his decision to forsake all to follow Elijah.

"God hasn't told me anything different," he might have thought. "So I'm going to go all the way with this service to the man of God. But I certainly am going to be more careful about what I say to him!"

The king of Israel did not give up easily. After all, he probably thought if he could get rid of the prophet, he could get rid of the sentence of death passed on him. He quickly sent another 50 men with their captain. And whoosh! Fire came down and consumed them also. (vv. 11,12.)

Elisha was learning things he had never known before and seeing things he had never seen before. He must have been startled. Perhaps he even considered going back to farming. But Elisha remembered that he had a "crowbar," and he began to use it.

Just like Elisha, often we go through a first fire and have to face another fire coming right behind it.

One Sunday morning, your pastor may speak pretty strong words from the pulpit. Perhaps he is calling on his members to straighten up their acts, come into unity with one another, and get on with the job. You immediately get hurt and defensive, but decide to give him another chance.

But the next Sunday, he does the same thing, calling forth an even stronger message. Alarmed, you suggest that your family leave the church and find another where the pastor brings messages of love from the pulpit. You need to remember Who said you should be in that church to begin with. Did you choose it, or did God?

Elisha was living through natural circumstances just as we have to do. Elijah never placed honors on him or certified his service. He did not make life easy for his servant. The servant's place was to make life easier for the man of God. Remember, Elisha wielded his crowbar and was not moved by the difficulty involved with serving the prophet. He simply went on serving.

Faithfulness Comes By Choice

Going through the fires of life can be easier if someone pats you on the back or reassures you of your calling. But the one thing that kept Elisha going was the fact that he had made a decision to serve, and he would be true to his word.

Everyone can get excited about being part of the supernatural or about following a great man of God. We might even dream of being Elijahs or Elishas, but we need to realize that life was not all roses for Elisha. We know the result of his years of service, but Elisha did not know until Elijah was taken up into the heavens.

Ahaziah was a stubborn man, especially with his life in the balance. He sent yet a third group of 50 men with a captain to take Elijah off the hill where he was sitting. But this captain had more common sense and wisdom than the previous two.

When he got to the hill where Elijah sat, he fell on his knees and pleaded for the lives of himself and his men. Then the angel of the Lord told Elijah it was time to go with the troops, so he came down off the hill and went to visit the king in person. (2 Kings. 1:13-15.)

These incidents were specialized training for Elisha. He used his crowbar and learned all of the lessons the Lord sent his way.

Ahaziah, king of Israel, soon found it had not done him any good to send after Elijah. When Elijah saw the king, he told him to his face the same thing he had said to the messengers:

> . . . **thou shalt not come down off that bed on which thou art gone up, but shalt surely die.**
>
> **2 Kings 1:16**

What happened to Elijah? The Bible does not tell us, but obviously, he walked out of the palace at Samaria a free man. In the very next chapter, we are told of his being taken up to heaven in a chariot of fire. We do know what happened to the king, because verse 17 says,

> **So he died according to the word of the Lord which Elijah had spoken.**

Elisha had to endure all kinds of surprises. But he stayed through it all, because he had made a decision. He continued to grow in every way as he abided by his word. Elisha had plenty of opportunities to bail out. If he had not been a man of his word, a man who stuck by his decisions, he would not have become the prophet who came after Elijah in the Bible. The prophet would have been someone else.

Elisha remained with the man of God whether he spoke judgment or blessings. Christians today get upset with those who bring correction from God or who carry "bad news." But nothing caused Elisha to waver. He used his special tool from God to stand by Elijah and to become personally all that God wanted him to be.

4

Molded, Shaped, and Prepared for God's Timing

The *crowbar* Elisha used was "faithfulness."

Faithfulness kept him at the prophet's side through every kind of adversity.

Faithfulness is the "crowbar of God."

Remember that Elisha was never told why he was to travel with Elijah. You have seen in the scriptures that his was not an easy life. Being in service to others means your life is not your own. There were fires to pass through and things to learn, all the while doing the menial, everyday tasks that go with living.

Do you think you could watch men be consumed by fire and still serve that prophet?

Finally, at the end of Elijah's life, we see Elisha's reward.

> And it came to pass, when the Lord would take up Elijah into heaven by a whirlwind, that Elijah went with Elisha from Gilgal.
>
> And Elijah said unto Elisha, Tarry here, I pray thee; for the Lord hath sent me to Beth-el. (Then Elisha began to use his crowbar.) And Elisha said unto him, As the Lord liveth, and as thy soul liveth, I will not leave thee. So they went down to Beth-el.
>
> 2 Kings 2:1,2

Elisha had feelings like us. Did he think, "Didn't the Lord say anything about me, Elijah? I've been with you for years; I've waited upon you hand and foot. Didn't God say anything about me?"

Even if he thought that, what he said was this: "Elijah, years ago the Lord called me, and I went with you as a servant. And, as long as I live, I am going to do what He said. I will stick with you wherever you go, no matter what."

The Scriptures say they both went down to Bethel. From a quick reading of the story, it may look as if Elijah is trying to shake Elisha off his trail. Was he trying to spoil God's plan? Was he trying to go alone?

No, Elijah was molding and shaping Elisha for something special yet to come. Elisha still did not know what the outcome of his life of service for Elijah would be. People today often say they know what the Lord has in store for them. Let me tell you something: They do not know what they are saying! They could not possibly know the plans of God in detail.

The Lord *does* give us general directions many times, and He *does* give us specific details occasionally. But if He laid out all of His plans for our lives in detail, we would not walk by faith. He would be denying us the exercising of our faith. And *it is impossible to please God* without faith! (Heb. 11:6.)

Elisha had been prepared, day by day for years, for a very special service. Elijah nurtured him in faithfulness from the very beginning.

Are you willing to let God shape and mold you for something more than what you know about?

Are you willing to let God use people — men of God — to do some of the molding and shaping?

Or are you going to bail out at the first fire, or get your feelings bruised when the prophet says, "The Lord told *me* to go to Bethel, not *you*."

Are you going to be left behind?

Sometimes we excuse ourselves for disobedience in leaving the church where God put us by these kinds of excuses: "Brother Bell, I'll tell you why I don't go to that church anymore. They put a new department head over me, and I'll tell you what, that guy rubs me the wrong way!"

I would like to answer, "Well, my good friend, you must need rubbing on those wrong ways of yours, or God would not have allowed that man to be put over you!"

So, yes, you may have a glimpse of the future, but you do not have nearly the full picture. If you told me what you were going to be doing six months from now, you would just be guessing at it. The only One Who knows what is going to be happening six months from now is God, and possibly, the men of God, His prophets.

God is good. He knows what He is doing. Are you willing to let Him have His way with you? Are you willing to let Him prepare you for service?

> **And the sons of the prophets that were at Beth-el came forth to Elisha, and said unto him, Knowest thou that the Lord will take away thy master from thy head to-day? And he said, Yea, I know it; hold ye your peace.**
>
> **2 Kings 2:3**

In other words, Elisha said, "I know what is going on, and I know what I'm doing. Just be quiet."

Those were the "sons (students) of the prophets." Those men were not "flakes." They knew what they were talking about. And you thought you could only be tempted by evil things?

What happens when your good Christian friends come and tell you of a new church starting up? These are people you respect; they are born again and filled with the Holy Spirit. They even prophesy now and again. Are you going to follow them? Or are you going to follow the man of God you were called to follow?

Times of Decision

You have to make a decision at times like these. Are you going to stay where God put you, or are you going to try to please your friends? Elisha made a decision, but as you can see, it was not a one-time decision in practice. He had to keep reaffirming his decision throughout all of those years.

When they got to Bethel, Elijah "tried" his servant again.

He said, "Okay, you followed me this far, but you stay here now. I have to go on to Jericho. The Lord has sent me to Jericho."

Elisha once again used that crowbar of faithfulness. Once again, he reaffirmed his decision to follow the prophet. He insisted on going with Elijah to Jericho.

Many Christians think they are to mold and shape themselves. Perhaps by attending Bible school, they will come out finished products for the Lord's use. But it does not take faith to mold yourself. Molding yourself is "works" — that is flesh

Are you willing to use the crowbar of faith, deal with one day at a time, and let a man of God shape you for something that only God knows about?

Once at Jericho, Elisha again was approached by students at the school of prophets there. They asked him the same thing the others did: Did he know his master is being taken up by God that day? Elisha gave them the same answer. He seemed to be pounded with trials right to the very end, being tested by those who were good people and friends. But this was all part of the shaping and molding process.

Then Elijah said to Elisha for the third time, "You stay here now. I have to go on to the Jordan River."

Elisha had not yet been told why he was following the man of God to the very end, but he knew he would not let go. He would not leave him until God took him. Elisha was using his crowbar of faithfulness that had been developed over his years of service.

And the two men, prophet and servant, went on. Verse 7 tells us that 50 sons of the prophets followed them and watched from a distance as they reached the river. They did what a lot of our well-meaning friends do. They try to stop us from doing what God is leading us to do, because they think we are wrong.

If someone wrote to you today and sent you a check for several thousand dollars to go to Bible school, would you pack up the next day and leave? Would you automatically think because this seems like a good thing that it is God's will? Would you even consider that God already had told you something else to do for Him?

Elijah took off his mantle, folded it together, and slapped the waters of the river with it. Second Kings, chapter 2, verse 8 says the river parted, and the two men walked across on dry land — as the Israelites had when they left Egypt just a jump ahead of Pharoah's army.

How would you react if you were standing there with Elijah? The prophet had called fire down from heaven, raised a boy from the dead, made the rain stop and begin again, and killed false prophets. He moved in the supernatural. So I am sure the parting of the waters of Jordan was no big deal to Elijah.

Then Elijah and Elisha walked across the dry riverbed. Elisha used his crowbar of faithfulness, telling himself that if the prophet was going, so was he. If the water came down, it would come down on both of them.

Pastors often strike the waters of a "faith venture" much to the surprise of their congregations. And they urge the whole church to come on through the "river," but many cannot make it. The waters are around them, and they shake and quake until they finally turn back.

A church can be very much like the man who set out to swim across the Mississippi River. He swam halfway, then decided he could not make it, so he turned around and swam back! He could have made it just as easily on across, but he chose to turn back. He gave up too soon.

When the man of God shows the way, you need to grab hold of his coattails and say, "You parted the waters. I'm sticking with you. If the water comes down, it will come down on both of us."

That is the force of faithfulness. Nothing can stop it.

Now look at the next verse:

> And it came to pass, when they were gone over, that Elijah said unto Elisha, Ask what I shall do for thee, before I be taken away from thee (v. 9a.)

Notice that Elisha did not react the way we may think. He was not jumping up and down, shouting, and carrying on. He answered, very humbly, **I pray thee** (please), **let a double portion of thy spirit be upon me** (v. 9b). Elisha asked this with a reverence and a fear of God. What he was about to ask for, no other man had ever asked for. I am sure that he did not even know if he would live to tell of this favor.

Elijah answered:

> Thou hast asked a hard thing: nevertheless, if thou see me when I am taken from thee, it shall be so unto thee; but if not, it shall not be so (v. 10).

Looking at the closing of Elijah's days on earth, we see a very important concept in becoming who God wants you to be, and that is *His timing*.

Elijah was saying, "Elisha, be faithful, and in the Lord's timing, you will receive your request for a double anointing."

"You can have it in the Lord's timing" might be a bit hard for you, a modern Christian, to swallow. So even at the price of irritating you, I will ask you to consider this again:

Are you willing to let God shape you, mold you, and prepare you so you can be ready for that time in your life?

Are you willing to step into the faith realm and let God and the man of God (your pastor) shape and mold you into God's precious pottery?

Elisha kept a good attitude, even after all of the things he had gone through, all of the serving, all of the frustration over the previous years. None of that affected Elisha's attitude toward his master (pastor). He could have decided not to even talk to him anymore — to just let the old guy go at it alone.

There had been a cultivation process in Elisha. The man of God, Elijah, had done his job well. He had molded and prepared his servant for ministry. He did his job so well that Elisha would do even greater supernatural feats than his teacher. Elijah could leave, knowing his ministry was in good hands.

> **And it came to pass, as they still went on, and talked, that, behold, there appeared a chariot of fire, and horses of fire, and parted them both asunder; and Elijah went up by a whirlwind into heaven.**
>
> **And Elisha saw it, and he cried, My father, my father, the chariot of Israel, and the horsemen thereof. And he saw him no more: and he took hold of his own clothes, and rent them in two pieces** (vv. 11,12).

In the Old Testament, it is unusual for the word *father* to be used in this manner, as a term of endearment. The man of God had shown him so many things, and they had grown so close over the years, that Elijah had really become like a father to Elisha. One of the many definitions of *pastor* is "father-like one." Suddenly, the man who always knew what was going on and what was to be done, had left Elisha without companionship and the security that comes with leaning on another in authority.

The Scriptures tell us, however, that Elisha then took up the mantle of Elijah, walked back to the river bank, and smote the waters just as his "father-like one" had done. He had grown in faithfulness. His "crowbar" had become a tool for success, and God's timing now rested on him.

Faithfulness Keeps You Humble

If you want faithfulness to take over in your life, then allow God to use the people set over you to form you into something useful. Start by being faithful where you are, in the little things. Make a decision, and be a man or woman of your word.

Elisha's faithfulness took over in his life. He had grown to the place where nothing else mattered. His faithfulness was in control. Now he had the mantle of the "father-like one," and as he hit the water, he said, **Where is the Lord God of Elijah?** (2 Kings 2:14).

The "Lord God of Elijah" answered him, the waters parted, and Elisha went back over the Jordan to where the sons of the prophets waited.

He remembered all that he had learned in his service to Elijah and walked on, now entered into his own ministry. When God is leading you to do something, He usually tells you just enough to get you going in the right direction. You are always required to trust Him and have faith in Him. God will tell you when to start using the crowbar He has given you.

Pry yourself out of that easy chair to go to church on Sunday and on week nights. Let God shape and mold you into what He wants. You have specialties for Him that only you can give Him. You will find God's will for your life with the help of your crowbar and your pastor. The crowbar belongs to you, however. Your pastor cannot use it for you. Only you can keep yourself in faith.

Years from now, the Lord may lead you in another direction. But for now, serve in your church. When you get into tomorrow, you are not in faith. Faith is now. Faith is for today. Christianity is exciting! You do not know what may happen from one day to the next.

If you are bored with your Christian walk, perhaps you are trying to mold and shape yourself. Faith is the thing that pleases God. And when you charge up with faith, things begin to move and happen. The boredom will leave as you serve.

Once, I wanted to leave a church where God had put me. There were many occasions when I wanted to leave, because I did not understand the things the pastor did to me. I would cry on my wife's shoulder about why "they" did not think I was faithful and why "they" were always testing my faithfulness.

Then I would remember the day in a church service when God seemed to open up and pour His supernatural love down on the inside of me. A mantle was dropped on me, and I could not sit in church anymore. I had to be involved. I did whatever I was asked to do. I was laughed at and mocked. I wanted to quit a thousand times, but I am a man of my word. I would not quit.

People would ask me, "Buddy, when are you going to leave the church and start your own ministry? You have *such* an anointing."

That was soothing to my ears at first, especially when the pastor had pointed his finger at me for doing something wrong. Then it sounded real good! But I was reminded of Elisha's saying **as the Lord liveth, and as thy soul liveth** (2 Kings 2:2), and I would reaffirm my resolve to serve my pastor. That was where God wanted me, in order to mold and shape me into what He wanted me to be.

God is the Potter, and we are the clay. Surrendering completely to His molding and shaping is scary sometimes and not always enjoyable. Somehow, we always feel we can do the job much better — although we *know* that we cannot.

But we are not to run our lives on the way we feel, but on what the Word of God says.

You can make the same decision I did: not to run anymore. You will find a peace, a joy, and more faithfulness than you have ever dreamed of from making that decision. You just need to grab your "crowbar." It is there, ready-made just for you. You will be staying under the anointing of the ministry of helps, and you have the ability to do supernatural things.

Second Kings 3:11,12 says:

> **But Jehoshaphat said, Is there not here a prophet of the Lord, that we may enquire of the Lord by him? And one of the king of Israel's servants answered and said, Here is Elisha the son of Shaphat, which poured water on the hands of Elijah** (who was the servant of that great man of God, Elijah).
>
> **And Jehoshaphat said, The Word of the Lord is with him . . . .**

Elisha: the one who was faithful!

5

No Big Guns and Little Guns

One day, I used the phrase, "big guns and little guns in the Body of Christ" in a sermon.

Instantly, the Holy Spirit stopped me and said, "There *are* no big guns and little guns. There is only *one* gun, and you are all bullets in it."

A few days later, he added to that statement by saying, "Often, when I pull the trigger, a lot of you don't go off." We have more clicks than bangs in the church.

Many Christians tend to think of the Church as having two rooms, one with helps and governments, and the other with apostles, prophets, evangelists, pastors, and teachers. Most of us think we want to be in that second room. We think that room is where it is all happening. We also think if we get in that first room, we will get caught and never get out.

There are not two rooms in the Church! There is only one. There is not a division in the Body of Christ. There is only one body. There are no "big guns and little guns," but one Gun, the Body of Christ.

Is the Ministry of Helps Biblical?

When they first begin to hear about a "ministry of helps," some people wonder if that is in the Bible.

One brother said, "You know if there is any new-fangled doctrine, it comes out of Tulsa, Oklahoma."

Christians today, want to know they are really part of the Church. They want to be participants, not spectators.

They want to know they are really part of their churches. When they are involved in the ministry of helps, they will *know* they are a part of their churches.

Look at the Apostle Paul's first letter to the church at Corinth.

> **And God hath set some in the church, first apostles, secondarily prophets, thirdly teachers, after that miracles, then gifts of healings, *helps*, governments, diversities of tongues.**
>
> **1 Corinthians 12:28**

Right there in the Word of God, it says *helps*. No man made it up. No committee put it into the church. This is not a "new-fangled doctrine" out of Tulsa.

The word *help(s)* is the Greek word *antilepsis*, or *antilempsis*, which means "a laying hold of, an exchange," or "to lay hold of, so as to support."[1]

In other words, if you are helping anyone in the church, or helping the weak or needy, you are operating in the ministry of helps, a "gift" set in the Church by God. This is a ministry just as valid, just as anointed, as if God had asked you to be a prophet. God is not a respecter of persons, nor should we be.

An usher, a nursery worker, a sound man, a musician, anyone giving assistance in the Body, is in the ministry of helps.

> Oh! The infinite value of the humble gospel helpers. Thousands of people who have no gifts as leaders are number-one helpers. How grand revival work moves along when red-hot platoons of fire-baptized helpers crowd around God's heroic leaders of the embattled hosts![2]

---

[1] W. E. Vine, *Vine's Expository Dictionary of Old and New Testament Words* (Old Tappan: Fleming H. Revell Company, 1981), Volume 2, p. 213.

[2] Rev. W. B. Godbey, *Godbey's Commentary* (Cincinnati: Revivalist Press. Copyright © 1986 by M. W. Knapp.)

Their task is just as important as those of people in leadership offices. God's rewards are not based on the size of the ministry on earth, but on the degree of faithfulness. Using the crowbar of faithfulness will bring you as many rewards in heaven for sweeping floors — if that is where God put you — as it will for building the biggest church in the country.

Faithfulness Makes the Difference

Faithfulness is necessary to everyone in the helps ministries. Take nursery workers: The first thing many parents say when they come to pick up their children is, "Boy, did we have a great service! You really missed it!" To some, the nursery room is the "missed-it" room!

I would not blame nursery workers for wanting to give up their helps ministries. Would it be the same if parents came to nursery workers and expressed appreciation for their being willing to miss the service and take care of the children for the Lord's sake?

Why do we place a higher regard, a higher honor, on some offices than others, when God does not?

If you are rendering assistance in any way inside or outside of your church walls, you are operating in the supernatural ministry of helps. The ministry of helps is as anointed as the calling of a prophet.

An usher shared this definition with me once, and my mouth just dropped open: *Helps* is spelled "H" — having, "E" — enough, "L" — loving, "P" — people, "S" — serving. *Helps* is "Having Enough Loving People Serving" in the church. I want to be one of those loving people who serves.

Romans 12:1 says:

> **I beseech you therefore, brethren, by the mercies of God, that ye present your bodies a living sacrifice, holy, acceptable unto God, which is your reasonable service.**

God is looking for living sacrifices. Some churches are full of dead sacrifices. But God is looking for people who are alive. It is not a hard thing to serve God. It is not a hard thing to be a **living sacrifice.** Only you and I make it hard. God does not make it hard.

> **And be not conformed to this world: but be ye transformed by the renewing of your mind, that ye may prove what is that good, and acceptable, and perfect, will of God.**
>
> **Romans 12:2**

Remember when you became a Christian how everything changed? Most of us changed the way we acted, the people we spent time with, the places we went, even sometimes, the clothes we wore. Are you starting to slip back to the way you were? Are you losing your first love?

> **For I say, through the grace given unto me, to every man that is among you, not to think of himself more highly than he ought to think; but to think soberly, according as God hath dealt to every man the measure of faith.**
>
> **Romans 12:3**

I am tired of hearing how five percent of the people in the Church do 90 percent of the work. It should be the other way around. So if you are an usher or a nursery worker, you should be praising the Lord.

When you begin to serve God, you step between the hands of God. He begins to shape and mold you. When you move, God moves. When you sit, God sits. He has not overlooked anyone in the Body of Christ. All of us have the same measure of faith, and every one of us is a *necessary* part of the Body.

How Important Is the Helps Ministry?

In a lot of churches where I teach ministry of helps seminars, I hear why first-time visitors often do not return — only many times I hear the wrong "reason." Most of the time, members blame it on the pastor.

I usually say, "You go out to the parking lot, get out of your car the way a visitor would, and come in here looking at and experiencing everything a visitor would, and we could see several reasons why you would not come back. That is *before* you even see the pastor, let alone hear him."

Visitors are moved by what they see, what they smell, what they hear, and so forth. First-time visitors usually are moved by their five senses: sight, hearing, taste, touch, and smell. The Queen of Sheba came to see King Solomon bearing great gifts, apparently in some skepticism concerning all she had heard. Second Chronicles 9:4 shows us how she was affected, when she had *seen* certain things.

> And the meat of his table, and the sitting of his servants, and the attendance of his ministers, and their apparel; his cupbearers also, and their apparel; and his ascent by which he went up into the house of the Lord; *there was no more spirit in her.*

I believe leaders should be examples. There are some things a leader might have done in the past that he cannot get away with anymore — this comes with the package. For example, a leader cannot be late to a service although he might have been able to get away with this when he was an usher (although being late is not right). A leader cannot get away with things like this because he is before the people more. But if he tries to, he had better build his cross because the people will nail him to it.

A friend of mine pastored a church in Charleston, West Virginia. He did something that was unusual in the Church at large. He had all of his church elders up on the platform with him during the entire service. So one day, I asked him why he did that.

He said, "The leadership here in the church is an example to the flock, and they are here to help me. Not everyone knows who the elders are, but the people need to take problems to the elders first. Then, if the elders can't handle them, they bring them to me. But, to do that, the people need to know who the elders are."

Then he added, "The people need to see the leadership praising and worshiping God. *People never go beyond their leadership.* There are some in leadership who are so good at hiding among the sheep that they could skip a service, and the sheep not even know they were not there. And, often, even the shepherds don't know the elders are not there!"

He shared with me, "I had to let one of my elders go once, and I had very little problem with the congregation over it. They had already *seen* that he did not even want to be there or do his job."

Apparel

Another thing someone shared with me once is this: He came into a church and could tell no difference between the people in church and the people in the street in their appearances, actions, and attitudes.

Some would say you have to dress like the world and look like the world to win them. However, that is not true. You do not win people because you look like them or smell like them. You win people because you have something better than the world can give them.

Another way people in the ministry of helps communicate is through body expression. Eighty-five percent of first impressions come through what the world calls "body language." Usually, you can tell what kind of week your pastor has had by the way he walks up to the podium. We are not to be conformed to this world. We are called to be different.

The Queen of Sheba said:

> . . . It was a true report which I heard in mine own land of thine acts, and of thy wisdom:

> **Howbeit I believed not their words, until I came, and mine eyes had seen it: and, behold, the one half of the greatness of thy wisdom was not told me: for thou exceedest the fame that I heard.**
>
> 2 Chronicles 9:5,6

What kind of reports are people hearing about your church? Are they true reports, or just reports? A report may be true, or it may be either a watered-down version of the truth, a distorted version of the truth, or an out-and-out falsehood. If people are hearing true reports, one day they will come to visit. True reports fuel curiosity!

Attitudes Are Very Revealing

Christians have been misled. We have been told that if you tell the world what it is really like in the Church, they will not come. So we water down the teaching of the Bible and the truths about the Christian life. Tell it like it is. When Peter and John were thrown in jail, it was not for preaching, but for telling people what they had seen and heard about Jesus.

Attitude was the other thing that affected Sheba's queen when she first visited Solomon. She saw that his men and his servants that stood "continually" before him were happy. (v. 7.) Everyone was happy. That told a lot about Solomon's style of kingship and about the conditions of the country.

At a typical church, a lot of first-time visitors come to the door to be greeted by people who may not look happy. Many door greeters are there because a pastor has heard he should have them. Door greeters should be people who pray and who genuinely are glad to see everyone who comes through the church doors. That kind of welcome makes all the difference.

Then the visitor who has children gets to the nursery. Some places, the nursery worker has parents fill out a lot of forms and almost sign in blood. Other places, the workers act as if keeping the nursery is a big favor — not a service — to the parents.

Then they might say, "Since you're new here, you ought to know we are not able to supply diapers for your baby, and we are not a babysitting service. As soon as church is over, please come and get your child."

After that, the visitor moves into the auditorium where the back wall has stood up all by itself for the previous six days, but now on Sunday morning, it seems to take all the deacons and ushers to hold it up. If an usher moves, he may point the visitor to the front seats. Usually, visitors like to sit in the back, not knowing where the regular members have their favorite seats and not wanting to draw attention to themselves.

Then the members come in and give visitors dirty looks because visitors are in the members' regular seats in the back row!

Perhaps the worship leader comes out and says, "Well, I'm glad to see somebody showed up this morning!"

So Dad and Mom look at each other and say, "Do you want to leave now, or do you want to wait until the preacher begins?"

And we wonder why people do not come back after visiting our churches. At this point in the service, it cannot be the preaching. Usually, they have made up their minds before the preacher even gets to the platform.

Then there is the other kind of church:

• The greeters genuinely seem glad to see visitors.

• The nursery worker welcomes the children, comforts and reassures them.

• The ushers have had a revelation from God that on the seventh day, the wall will still stand.

• The worship leader comes out ready to praise and worship and brings the people together in a spirit of praise.

Even before the visitors see the pastor, they know this is a happy church. This is a church where people love one another.

The pastor can preach the most anointed sermon in the world, but if the people in the helps ministry are not doing their jobs in love and not showing Jesus to other people, visitors will not want to come back.

Your church does not belong to your pastor and his wife. They are not the Body, only part of it. The congregation is the larger part of the Body in your church. Those in the five ministry offices are there to perfect the saints (all believers) in order for the saints to do the work of the ministry. (Eph. 4:12.)

What is the work of the ministry? Winning souls and showing people how to live in the Kingdom of God. We are all in this together.

6

Prerequisite for a Victorious Ministry

Not slothful in business; fervent in spirit; serving the Lord.

Romans 12:11

Several years ago, I came to a place in my life and in my Christian walk where confusion began to interfere with my progress. The confusion was in the area of *zeal*. I noticed that a lot of people did not understand zeal. Some Christians acted as if zeal were a disease.

In Romans 12:11, the word *fervent* means "zealous." So the Bible says that we need to have zeal in serving the Lord.

But many times Christians would tell me I was full of zeal, and then they would back up as if I had something they did not want. You say *zeal* in some churches, and it is as if you said a dirty word.

When I began to look into this subject, however, I discovered a lot of people do not know what zeal is. They think zeal means bouncing off the walls and rolling on the floor. That is not zeal.

I know other Christians who seem to pick and choose what parts of God they want. But how can you pick and choose? I want *all* of God.

Then, I heard a preacher say that the zeal of God is like a consuming fire. I know that nothing could stand against the fire of God, and I know that the devil will try to put this and that on me. But if I stay full of the zeal of God, those things cannot stay on me. Nothing can stand against the fire of God.

I have watched congregations singing about the zeal of God coming over them and burning in their souls, but you could see from their faces they were just singing words. They had no revelation of the words they were singing. In my visits to churches, the most people I have found in one place who understood the zeal of God was six.

One day, I decided to find out what the Bible says about *zeal*. I believe it is time for Christians to take zeal out of their spiritual closets, shake the dust off it, and apply it in their lives.

What Does the Bible Say About Zeal?

For he put on righteousness as a breastplate, and an helmet of salvation upon his head; and he put on the garments of vengeance for clothing, and was clad with zeal as a cloak.

Isaiah 59:17

That verse is part of a prophecy about Jesus, and the prophet said that the Messiah would put on *zeal* like a coat. He would cover Himself with zeal. Did Jesus not know it was wrong to have zeal? Did He not know He would be considered a second-class citizen if He walked around in zeal?

After reading just that one verse, I wondered where people got the idea that zeal was something suspicious and undesirable.

Psalm 119:139 says:

My zeal hath consumed me, because mine enemies have forgotten thy words.

How many of us today could stand up and say our zeal for the cause of Christ has consumed us?

Look at Isaiah 9:6,7:

> For unto us a child is born, unto us a son is given: and the government shall be upon his shoulder: and his name shall be called Wonderful, Counsellor, The Mighty God, The everlasting Father, The Prince of Peace.
>
> Of the increase of his government and peace there shall be no end, upon the throne of David, and upon his kingdom, to order it, and to establish it with judgment and with justice from henceforth even for ever. The zeal of the Lord of hosts will perform this.

Do you want the government to be established on the shoulders of Jesus Christ? I do. Some inroads have been made into turning our government around, but there is something missing. The last part of that verse says the *zeal* of the Lord will perform this.

That is what is missing today — the zeal of the Lord of hosts. Why do we back away from it in the Church?

Isaiah 63:15 should be the prayer of the Church:

> Look down from heaven, and behold from the habitation of thy holiness and of thy glory: where is thy zeal and thy strength, the sounding of thy bowels and of thy mercies toward me? are they restrained?

Where is the zeal of God in the Church today? Nobody knows, and some are glad it is not around.

Why Are We Afraid of Zeal?

Why is the Body of Christ afraid of the zeal of God? Perhaps we ought to look at some verses that have been used to throw zeal out of the church.

> Brethren, my heart's desire and prayer to God for Israel is, that they might be saved.
>
> For I bear them record that they have a zeal of God, but not according to knowledge.
>
> For they being ignorant of God's righteousness, and going about to establish their own righteousness, have not submitted themselves unto the righteousness of God.
>
> Romans 10:1-3

Did Paul write that it is wrong to have zeal?

Did he write that all Christians need to get rid of zeal, that all we need is knowledge?

Misunderstanding those verses is one reason Christians say, "You're just full of zeal. You need the Word of God."

What Paul was saying is this: "My brethren have a zeal toward God but they do not have the right knowledge to base that on. They are trying to work out the zeal of God in their own righteousness instead of in His."

Their *knowledge* was what was wrong, not their zeal. In earlier Church times, we had the zeal, but somewhere along the way, Christians decided it was time to put zeal aside and get hold of the Word of God. Get knowledge! Now, all the "knowledge" people are sitting around saying something is missing. They have been getting hold of the Word of God for years, and there is still something missing.

Paul did not say to get rid of one and go after the other. What would happen if we put zeal and knowledge together?

Remember when you got saved? Remember when you first were a Christian? You could not wait for the church doors to open. You were on fire. You were hot. Then along came Brother and Sister Knowledge, and you began to grow cold.

I was out driving in Tulsa, Oklahoma, near our home once with my four daughters, when one of them yelled, "Daddy, look at that flag. Look how big it is! It's an American flag, too!"

I looked, and I noticed that the flag was just hanging there. It was not doing anything. God does not want us to let our zeal "flag," waiting for some circumstance, some outside influence, to come along and blow on it.

Are you "just hanging there"? What about when the wind comes up? Do not be satisfied just to be a "flag" for God. *You* are in control. Maintain your spiritual glow. Zeal is not some weird thing that might get on you. Zeal means serving the Lord with an energetic spirit. Some translations say to keep the fires of the spirit burning.

Who Keeps Zeal Intact?

All of that sounds as if it is our responsibility to keep the zeal of God intact and alive in us.

> Epaphras, who is one of you, a servant of Christ, saluteth you, always labouring fervently for you in prayers, that ye may stand perfect and complete in all the will of God.
>
> For I bear him record, that he hath a great zeal for you, and them that are in Laodicea, and them in Hierapolis.
>
> Colossians 4:12,13

Where do people come up with this teaching that it is wrong to have zeal? Where do they get this idea that zeal is a part of God you really do not want?

> Looking for that blessed hope, and the glorious appearing of the great God and our Saviour Jesus Christ;
>
> Who gave himself for us, that he might redeem us from all iniquity, and purify unto himself a peculiar people, zealous of good works.
>
> Titus 2:13,14

Are you part of a peculiar people? Jesus is coming after a peculiar people *zealous* of good works. Can you imagine a big bus that comes down from heaven, the door opens, and out steps an angel who says:

"May I have your attention please? Would all of you who are just peculiar please step to the left? Now, you that are peculiar *and* zealous of good works, I would like for you to get on, and we'll take right off. You that are just peculiar, we might be back."

I was preaching this in one church, and just as I came to the part about the bus, a bus pulled up outside. Some of the people broke out into a sweat! You could see them thinking, "Hurry up and tell us, Brother Bell! What is it? The bus has arrived!" Well, we have some time yet before this bus arrives.

Look at what Jesus said in Revelation 3:19:

As many as I love, I rebuke and chasten: be zealous therefore, and repent.

Did Jesus not know that *zeal* is a "no-no"? For almost ten years, I have been in hundreds of churches, and I have noticed something. Not only is there little zeal; there is very little repentance going on.

You say, "I don't have to come forward to repent. God meets me at my chair."

But when you repent, you turn 180 degrees and go the other way. Genuine repentance brings change. But people do not come to the altar anymore. Sometimes, churches do not even have altars. I have heard people say that years ago, the altars always were full. Christians were on their knees repenting. People are not repenting today because there is little zeal in the Church. Many Christians do not know what the zeal of God is.

When I got to this place in my study of zeal, I made up my mind and said in my heart that Buddy Bell would never again deny the zeal of God. It was settled in my heart that I would never stand still and be quiet when a Christian pointed out other Christians and criticized their zeal. Yet I could not tell you what zeal was.

Zeal in a Nutshell

One day as I was riding in the back seat of a car headed for a meeting, I was thinking about zeal. I was not ready to teach on it yet, because I did not have a full understanding. But I was meditating on these scriptures and definitions.

And I said, "Lord, would You just put it into a nutshell for me? What is Your zeal?"

The Lord said, "Buddy, My zeal is a never-quitting attitude. Jesus surrounded Himself with a never-quitting attitude."

The Word of God says that the government would be established on the shoulders of Jesus by a *never-quitting* attitude in the Body of Christ. We cannot quit! We need to be able to say that we are consumed by a never-quitting attitude.

Jesus is coming for a peculiar people, a people with a never-quitting attitude toward good works. Allow the zeal of God to come up on the inside of you. Do not quit!

When I began to travel and hold seminars in churches and auditoriums, something began to happen that at first I would not tell anyone for fear they would think I had "flipped out." If a meeting did not go quite right, I would go back to the motel, look at myself in the mirror, and say:

"Buddy Bell, get it together. You are going to do what God wants you to do. You are going to go where God wants you to go. You are going to be what God wants you to be. You are not going to quit."

After I did this study on zeal, I realized it was the zeal of God rising up inside me that caused me to do that. That was zeal rising up to consume me. When I am consumed with that never-quitting attitude, there is nothing the devil can throw at me to stop me.

You need knowledge, but do not throw away the zeal. Without zeal, knowledge will not be of much value. Catch hold of the zeal of God, and your helps ministry will be victorious. Have a zeal for what God has set you to do, and it will be easy to be obedient and faithful in it. You cannot fulfill your calling in the helps ministry without zeal.

Part Two:
The Ministry of Helps
Study Course

7

Introduction:
How To Use the Study Course

The Ministry of Helps Study Course is designed to help the believer understand in greater depth the truths brought forth in the Word of God concerning the ministry of helps.

This program of study is based on outlines that I use in teaching a three-day seminar on this subject.

The study course in this book includes three weeks of study materials with five lessons a week, one for each day. To gain the most from this study, you should complete *only* one lesson each day.

After each lesson, you will find several questions. Answer each one carefully, taking time to think before you answer. The questions are designed to teach you how to meditate in God's Word.

You *meditate* on a teaching by carefully considering each important point of the lesson. Make sure you understand in your heart what the Holy Spirit has brought to *you* specifically.

According to David, king and psalmist, those who *meditate* in God's Word day and night are the ones who will prosper in this life.

> But his delight is in the law of the Lord; and in his law doth he *meditate* day and night.
>
> And he shall be like a tree planted by the rivers of water, that bringeth forth his fruit in his season; his leaf also shall not wither; and whatsoever he doeth shall prosper.
>
> **Psalm 1:2,3**

The Hebrew word *hagah* translated in this psalm as *meditate* means "to murmur, to mutter . . . to meditate, to muse, to speak, to praise; to whisper."[1] The Biblical *meditate* obviously does not have the meaning common usage gives it today, that of sitting quietly, or, in some cases, even going into a trance-like state of mind.

To be certain you have all of the illumination or revelation the Holy Spirit wants you to have out of these lessons, praise the Lord after you study and thank Him for His Word. Then read the lessons out loud and consider them. Find any scriptures that come to your mind, or are given along with the lesson, and mentally "chew" them over as a cow chews her cud.

If you will take these lessons seriously and with a teachable spirit, this course will help you prosper in the ministry of helps.

---

[1] Spiros Zodhiates, *The Greek-Hebrew Key Study Bible* (Grand Rapids: Baker Book House, AMG Publishers, 1984), p. 1587.

8

Lesson One:
What *Is* the Ministry of Helps?

Day One: Defining the Ministry of Helps

> And God hath set some in the church, first apostles, secondarily prophets, thirdly teachers, after that miracles, then gifts of healings, helps, governments, diversities of tongues.
>
> 1 Corinthians 12:28

The ministries that we call "the five-fold offices," are to help the Church grow. However, all of the jobs designated by the Lord must be done if God's goal for His family is to be reached.

If you are born again, you are part of God's family. As part of the family of God, have you ever wondered what your place might be in the family? Or have you ever wanted to be able to help your brothers and sisters in the Lord?

Do you have a desire to be part of God's mighty move in these last days?

God indeed has called you to a very important ministry — the ministry of helps. Notice in the verse above two "statements" the Holy Spirit made through the Apostle Paul about the helps ministry:

1. It is a supernatural ministry, listed among things such as miracles and healings.
2. It is a "gift" God has set in the Church like a concrete pillar to hold things up.

Who Do You Help?

You may be wondering, "If I am in the *helps ministry,* who do I help?

You help the one God has set in each church to oversee it. Your job is to help your pastor run the church. Helps ministries act like fingers on a hand in assisting pastors.

The Lord has given your pastor a vision for his church, and He has given you to your pastor to "help" bring that vision to pass. Without the helps ministry, things will not get done. A pastor without those set help him would be like a hand without fingers.

Day Two: The Purpose of the Helps Ministry

And he gave some, apostles; and some, prophets; and some, evangelists; and some, pastors and teachers;

For the perfecting of the saints, for the work of the ministry, for the edifying of the body of Christ.

Ephesians 4:11,12

Have you ever wondered why God set apostles, prophets, evangelists, pastors, and teachers in the Church?

Paul made it clear in his letter to the church at Ephesus that the ministry gifts were put in the Body of Christ for one main purpose: to perfect (or mature) the saints.

People who are maturing, growing up in Christ, will exhibit two qualities:

1. They will build up and add to the welfare of God's family, the Church.

2. They will learn to minister — to help or serve — others.

You can tell the truly mature Christians in every situation by those who help the pastor, not hinder him.

Footnote: See study questions, Chapter 11.

Given the opportunity through your prayers and support, God will enable your pastor or pastors to equip and perfect you with everything you need to function supernaturally in the ministry of helps.

Day Three: One Who Gives Assistance

God himself set the ministry of helps in the Body of Christ, as we saw from 1 Corinthians 12:18. *Helps* is a supernatural ministry with its own supernatural anointing to serve God by serving His pastors and His people.

The definition of *helps* literally is "one who gives assistance."

If someone in your church needs help, and you can meet that need, do it! That will keep your pastor from having to do it.

Satan delights in keeping a pastor so busy that he cannot lead the people as he ought to do. Your obedience to God's call for the helps ministry will protect your pastor from this dangerous snare. God wants to speak to His people through the pastor, but He cannot if the pastor is too busy to spend time in prayer.

In Numbers 11:10-17, we read how God set the ministry of helps into His people of that day — Israel. Moses could no longer help the people individually. There were too many of them with too many problems.

Moses cried out to God about **the burden of all this people upon me** (v. 11), and God answered. The Lord told Moses to pick 70 elders of the people and bring them before Him. Then the Lord said He would **take of the spirit which is upon thee, and will put it upon them** (v. 17) in order that the elders might share the burden of the people.

The 70 elders were given a supernatural ability to share the load of caring for God's people. Doing the things that will benefit the pastor takes a supernatural anointing. Ask God for this anointing, and He will gladly answer. God's vision is the one He gave your pastor, so help the pastor fulfill that to the glory of the Lord.

Day Four: Not Everyone Is Called to an Apostle, Prophet, Teacher, Evangelist, or Pastor Office

When God calls people to work for Him, they usually assume He wants them to preach. However, God also calls people to sweep floors or work in the nursery.

Read 1 Corinthians 12:14-28. In those verses, the analogy used by the Apostle Paul to explain the Body of Christ was that of the human body. If one part is missing or malfunctioning, the body suffers loss and is handicapped.

God knew it would take many different ministries to keep a church family strong and healthy. If one failed, the others would suffer for it.

Another thing that is important to remember is that God sets each member where *He* wills, not where the member wills. God knows where you will be the most effective in caring for His people. When every part does its job, there is no division in the church body. You may not be the pastor, but God will give you a similar vision.

You *can* share in the effort to achieve that goal and share in the reward for helping the pastor accomplish God's commission. The helps ministry is a sort of apprenticeship program. When you prove yourself faithful and obedient in one job, God will promote you to another.

Day Five: The Disciples Had Helps Ministries

The best example of helps ministries in the Bible can be seen in the events of Jesus' life. He came to earth to live a natural life before God in such a way that we could imitate and follow it. Look at a few experiences Jesus had:

In Matthew 10:5-8, Jesus sent out the twelve disciples. Why did He not go Himself?

Like any other shepherd, Jesus was only one man. He could do only so much by Himself. God gave Him the ministry of helps to expand His ability to minister to the people in all of the towns and villages to which He went.

In Matthew 14:15-21, we read about Jesus multiplying the loaves and fishes to feed more than 5,000 people. How was the food distributed? He did it through the ministry of helps, just as any pastor today would have to do.

In Matthew 8:23-26, the apostle wrote of an incident when Jesus was asleep in the boat during a storm at sea that threatened to sink them. How could anyone sleep through a storm like that? Sleeping through a storm is easy when you are physically exhausted from preaching. The disciples were doing the rowing so that Jesus could get the rest He so badly needed.

Maybe this is a good reason for you to help your pastor. When the disciples got into trouble during the storm, Jesus was there to take charge and rebuke the storm. Your pastor will do the same for you, if you give him the chance to be the leader and shepherd. But he can only do this if you give him time to rest by doing the jobs he otherwise would have to do.

The ministry of helps also handled the Last Supper for Jesus. Read Mark 14:12-16.

Jesus made great use of the ministry of helps in His time. God's men and women today have the same problems handling everything that needs to be done that Moses and Jesus did. God wants to make the same use of the ministry of helps today that He did in times past.

9

Lesson Two:
The Work of the Ministry of Helps

Day One: The Strong Church

> But now hath God set the members every one of them in the body, as it hath pleased him.
>
> And whether one member suffer, all the members suffer with it; or one member be honoured, all the members rejoice with it.
>
> Now ye are the body of Christ, and members in particular.
>
> And God hath set some in the church, first apostles, secondarily prophets, thirdly teachers, after that miracles, then gifts of healings, helps, governments, diversities of tongues.
>
> 1 Corinthians 12:18,26-28

The ministry of helps is a supernatural ministry set in a church by God to help bring to pass the vision or goal God gave the pastor. The simple definition of helps is "one who gives assistance to the weak and needy."

In verse 18, we see that every member is put in the Church for a purpose. Every believer has a job to do in helping to care for God's people.

Verse 25 says, **...but that the members should have the same care one for another.** Caring for someone is not a mental attitude but an *action* whereby you watch out for the needs and welfare of others.

In verse 26, you can see that when you do not do your part, someone else suffers. When people are suffering, you should be there to comfort them. When they rejoice, you should be there to rejoice with them and spur them on. (Heb. 10:24.)

God never intended for any believer to be a pew sitter, week after week. He put you in your church to help. Where people do not help, the Body of Christ is weak.

Your church is made stronger when you are strong in the ministry of helps toward others. The Church is weak when everyone looks at a problem and says, "I wish someone would do something about that."

You are that someone set in the Church by God to do something about it!

Day Two: Order of Authority and God's Anointing

Read Numbers 11:10-17, which I wrote about earlier in these lessons. Moses was placed by God to oversee and care for His people, the Israelites. He was anointed to do the job and had God's ability to lead the people for the Lord.

As you see from those verses, a time came when the job was too big for one man. So God set the ministry of helps in the nation to assist Moses in caring for the people. Seventy elders were supernaturally empowered to assist and help Moses, the man with the vision. Those men then also had the vision for what Moses was doing and had the same heart to get it done.

The anointing of God came down through a definite order. God's anointing went to Moses; Moses' anointing flowed to the 70 called to help. God has the same order today. He gave all power to Jesus, Who sent the Holy Spirit, Who called and anointed the five-fold ministry. (Eph. 4:11.)

Where does the anointing go from there? To *you! You* are the one those men and women of God are to equip and perfect. (Eph. 4:12.)

Your pastor is sent by God to train you to work building up Christ's Body, the Church. The pastor does not build up the Church. He is supposed to train you to do it. Listen and learn from him, so God can use you in your own ministry. The pastor's vision and anointing will flow into you if you will let it.

God will enable you to do the job just as He did Moses' men and Jesus' disciples.

Day Three: Serving God's Chosen Man

In Exodus 24:13, God's chosen man had a minister. Joshua was called to minister to Moses. The word minister in that context does not mean "preacher" but "servant."

In a restaurant, the job of a waitress is to "minister" to you, to serve your table. Whatever your need is for that meal, she is to make sure it is met. What kind of waitress would she be if she never were around when you needed something? A good waitress watches carefully over your table and is there whenever you need her.

Joshua was chosen by God to wait on, or to serve, Moses. He was to help Moses by serving his needs so that Moses could keep his mind on God's work.

Joshua was the only one allowed to go with Moses to Mount Sinai and see the spectacular things of God that Moses saw. Why? Joshua was allowed to be involved at such a momentous time because he was a faithful servant to God's chosen man.

Being a servant was a menial thing to most people — and still is considered that way — but Joshua saw it as a ministry unto the Lord. Eventually, he was promoted to the position of leader of all Israel!

Your pastor will be more effective if he is not concerned with day-to-day duties such as sweeping the floor, mowing the lawn, or painting the church. The list is endless, and it puts an endless load on the pastor who does not have someone to help him, or her.

I would rather have my pastor before God in prayer and in the Word than have him sweeping the floor. I want him perfectly in tune with God so that he can minister to the people. In Acts 6:2,3, the apostles realized this:

> **Then the twelve called the multitude of the disciples unto them, and said, It is not reason that we should leave the word of God, and serve tables.**
>
> **Wherefore, brethren, look ye out among you seven men of honest report, full of the Holy Ghost and wisdom, whom we may appoint over this business.**

Day Four: Elisha, the Faithful Minister

In 2 Kings 2:1-15, we are told of Elijah, the prophet, as he came to the end of his ministry. God was preparing to take him home. When Elijah was gone, God would need someone else to carry on. Elisha was the man chosen by God for the job.

There are three things to notice about Elisha:

1. He served Elijah for a number of years.

2. He was faithful to the man with the vision.

3. He eventually was promoted.

Ten years is a long time to be following someone around, acting as his servant. But God knew what He was doing. Those years are what it took to mold and shape Elisha by experience into the kind of man God needed.

You may be thinking, "I have been here five years, and I am still a Sunday school teacher. When is God going to promote me?"

God will promote you when He knows you are ready to be promoted.

Just as Elisha was faithful to the man with the vision, you must prove yourself faithful to the man with the vision under whom God has set you.

Elisha not only was promoted in the end, but he received a double-portion of Elijah's anointing. He did twice as many miracles as Elijah.

Do not "put God in a box" regarding how long you serve a man of God. If you are faithful, God will promote you when He is ready and when you are ready.

Day Five: The Fruit of a Faithful Servant

You may think you are not qualified for the ministry of helps. However, you need to remember that it is God Who qualifies a person for a place of service in the Body of Christ. This *qualifying* is the supernatural part of the ministry of helps.

What then is the natural side, or your part in the helps ministry?

The one thing only you can supply to your ministry is *faithfulness*. God cannot make you faithful to His will and plan for your life. You must decide to be faithful and trustworthy. This is the main element you must bring into your ministry to God and to the Church.

The Bible has much to say about those who are faithful:

• In Proverbs 13:17, the faithful enjoy health. God blesses them with health and happiness because of their obedience.

• In Proverbs 25:13, a faithful servant is said to refresh his master. How would you like to be a blessing and a refreshing to your pastor? That is what God said a faithful servant would do.

• In Proverbs 28:20, God promises that the faithful servant will abound with blessings. Good things will come

79

his way. When you set your mind to see after your pastor's welfare, God will take care of yours.

• In Daniel 6:4, we see the testimony of the faithful servant. No fault or wrong can be found in him. There is nothing he can be accused of because he is right with God. Faithfulness will put you in a place of honor in the eyes of your pastor.

10

Lesson Three:
Having a Vision

Day One: You Must Have a Vision

> If any of you lack wisdom, let him ask of God, that giveth to all men liberally, and upbraideth not; and it shall be given him.
>
> But let him ask in faith, nothing wavering. For he that wavereth is like a wave of the sea driven with the wind and tossed.
>
> For let not that man think that he shall receive any thing of the Lord.
>
> A double minded man is unstable in all his ways.
> **James 1:5-8**

Double minded means you do not stick to one way of thinking. In the helps ministry, it refers to an individual who has received direction from God but keeps getting off the track.

If God has called you to help the pastor by being an usher, do not try to fill some other position. Wisdom from God belongs to the single-minded Christian who sticks to what God has given him until it is done. We must resist the temptation to get our fingers into other things.

God has given your pastor a vision for your church, and he is responsible to bring it to pass. However, he will need help. That is why God has placed you there: to be a minister of helps to your pastor so that the vision can be reached.

A vision is a goal and a direction from God, a divine guidance that God gives you. Put faith with corresponding action to bring it to pass.

Proverbs 29:18 says:

> **Where there is no vision, the people perish: but he that keepeth the law, happy is he.**

Christians without a vision die. They shrivel up like fruit that has been on the tree too long. Those who will receive, and act on, the part of the pastor's vision which God gives *them* to perform will experience the supernatural working of God in their lives.

Day Two: God Gives the Vision

> **(As it is written, I have made thee a father of many nations,) before him whom he believed, even God, who quickeneth the dead, and calleth those things which be not as though they were.**
>
> **Romans 4:17**

You can see that it was God Who gave Abraham the vision of becoming the father of many nations. Romans 4:18 calls that vision *hope.* When all hope of having a son was gone, God gave Abraham *supernatural hope.* On the other hand, another name for supernatural hope is *vision.* God showed Abraham what things would come to pass if he cooperated.

The Lord also has given your pastor hope, or a vision, for the future. There are four ways God gives people this kind of vision:

First, He could speak to your heart.

Second, He could give you an open vision — one you could see with your eyes.

Third, He might give you an inward vision.

Fourth, He might show you that vision in His Word.

Those who are called to the ministry of helps will have the same vision from God as the pastor. You may not get the vision the same way your pastor did, but God will put His vision in you as He sees fit.

Abraham received the fulfillment of his vision because he had faith in God's ability and willingness to do it. Paul tells us that we also must walk by faith and not by sight. (2 Cor. 5:7.) If we are faithful, God will bring that vision to pass; so have faith in the fulfillment of your vision.

In Proverbs 29:18, God said that people perish (fail) without a vision. Your church will fail without a vision on which you can put your faith.

Hebrews 11:1 says that faith gives substance (reality or existence) to things hoped for. If you have no hope or vision, then you have nothing to trust and believe God for; therefore, nothing will happen or come to pass in your life or the church.

God is in the hope-giving business, so when He speaks to you, listen to Him!

Day Three: Helping God's Man With the Vision

And it came to pass, when Moses held up his hand, that Israel prevailed: and when he let down his hand, Amalek prevailed.

But Moses' hands were heavy; and they took a stone, and put it under him, and he sat thereon; and Aaron and Hur stayed up his hands, the one on the one side, and the other on the other side; and his hands were steady until the going down of the sun.

Exodus 17:11,12

We can see the part that Moses' helpers played in overcoming Amalek. God told Moses how to win the battle, and Aaron and Hur helped. They did not win it, but they helped Moses win it.

God will always send people with the man of vision. If you want to be where things are happening in the Lord, join yourself to the man God sends you to and help him work toward the fulfillment of his vision.

God's will for your church is expressed in the vision or goal He has given to your pastor. Like Moses, your pastor will encounter times when he needs support to continue in the way the Lord has directed. Do not run ahead of him when he appears to be going too slow.

Sometimes we are quick to criticize a pastor for the way he is handling something. We need to remember that he is the man with the vision, the one God called to do it. Support your pastor's arms in the warfare with the enemy. See the supernatural move of the Lord.

You can be one who takes part in bringing about God's purpose in the land, if only you will learn to be like Aaron and Hur — simply content to hold up the arms of the man of vision, knowing he cannot make it unless you, or someone like you, holds up his arms.

Day Four: Being Knit Together

> So all the men of Israel were gathered against the city, *knit together as one man.*
>
> **Judges 20:11**

They were organized so that each man supported and protected the other. No man would fight alone, but rather with the combined force of the entire nation.

The Church has been called by God to be knit together as one body. Our success in this world depends on unity! The best way to beat an army is to scatter its soldiers — stop the unity! Satan wants to do that to your church. We are workers together with God. (1 Cor. 3:9.)

If you want to work with the Holy Spirit, you will have to work together with your brothers in the Lord, because that is who He is working with.

> Now I beseech you, brethren, by the name of our Lord Jesus Christ, that ye all speak the same thing, and that there be no divisions among you; but that ye be perfectly joined together in the same mind and in the same judgment.
>
> **1 Corinthians 1:10**

God's idea of unity includes everyone speaking the same thing, with no divisions — one in mind and opinion. These qualities produce one thing, shown in Genesis 11:1-6. God Himself said nothing would be impossible for the body of people that built the Tower of Babel. Why? He said that because of their unity. That is why He changed the one language of the world into many — to break up the unity of minds.

Jesus said in Matthew 18:19:

> **Again I say unto you, That if two of you shall agree on earth as touching any thing that they shall ask, it shall be done for them of my Father which is in heaven.**

God will work and move supernaturally among His people when they are in harmony together.

Day Five: The Helps Ministry in the Early Church

In Acts 6:1-7, you will see that the early Church had a ministry of helps that greatly aided the growth of Christianity in the world. There are seven things you need to notice about this event:

1. The Word of God increased (spread) after the ministry of helps was added to the Church.

2. Those in the helps ministry had hands laid upon them to receive the anointing to do the job.

3. The purpose was to give the men with the vision time for Bible study and prayer.

4. Stephen did mighty miracles because he had proven himself faithful in serving. Therefore, he was promoted by God to the miracle ministry.

5. Church growth resulted from the work of the helps ministry.

6. This demonstrates that God will add to your church as well, when He knows that you can care for them.

7. The people did not lay hands on those called, but the apostles did, as Christ's direct representatives of His authority on earth.

All of these things combined to produce a supernatural, growing Church that turned the world upside down. There is no reason we cannot do that again — if we learn from the experiences of those who made up the first-generation Church.

11

Study Questions

Chapter 8: Lesson One

Day One

1. What kind of list is given in 1 Corinthians 12:28?

_____

_____

_____

2. Who set "helps" in the Church?

_____

_____

_____

3. What was God's purpose in setting helps ministries in the Church?

_____

_____

_____

4. *Who* does the helps ministry help?

_____

_____

_____

5. What can happen to a church with no helps ministry?

_____

_____

_____

Day Two

1. What are the five ministry gifts in Ephesians 4:11?

_____

_____

_____

2. How many of these are gifts from God to the Church?

_____

_____

_____

3. What is the main purpose of these ministries in the Church?

_____

_____

_____

4. What is another word for *perfecting?*

   _____

   _____

   _____

5. What are the two qualities of those maturing in Christ?

   _____

   _____

   _____

6. How can you tell who the truly mature Christians are in the Church?

   _____

   _____

   _____

7. Who does God use to equip and perfect you for works of service to His Church?

   _____

   _____

   _____

8. Why did God give you a pastor in your church?

   _____

   _____

   _____

Day Three

1. What is the definition of the ministry of helps?

_____

_____

_____

2. What benefit does your pastor receive when you help others in the church?

_____

_____

_____

3. What does Satan delight in doing to pastors?

_____

_____

_____

4. Why did Moses cry out to God? (Num. 11:10-17.)

_____

_____

_____

5. How did God answer him?

_____

_____

_____

6. What did the Lord give the 70 elders of Israel whom Moses chose to help him?

    _____

    _____

    _____

7. In Numbers 11:17, what did God say was the *purpose* of the helps ministry to Moses?

    _____

    _____

    _____

Day Four

1. Who decides what job you will do in the Church?

    _____

    _____

    _____

2. Why does God set members in the Church as *He* wills?

    _____

    _____

    _____

3. What happens when all members do their parts? (1 Cor. 12:25.)

    _____

    _____

    _____

4. How does 1 Corinthians 12:14-28 apply to your church? What do those verses say to you?

    _____

    _____

    _____

5. What happens to those who share in the effort to bring to pass the pastor's God-given vision?

    _____

    _____

    _____

6. What would happen if everyone in your church decided to become a preacher?

    _____

    _____

    _____

Day Five

1. In Matthew 10:5-8, why did Jesus send out the disciples instead of going Himself?

    _____

    _____

    _____

2. How did Jesus manage to distribute food to the 5,000 in Matthew 14:15-21?

_____

_____

_____

3. In Matthew 8:23-26, there is another reason why Jesus needed the ministry of helps. What is it?

_____

_____

_____

4. Who made the preparations for the Last Supper?

_____

_____

_____

5. If you were to help your pastor as the disciples helped Jesus, what would happen in your church?

_____

_____

_____

Chapter 9: Lesson Two

Day One

1. What *kind* of ministry is the helps ministry?

_____

_____

_____

2. Why was the helps ministry set in the Church?

_____

_____

_____

3. How many members are set in the Church by God? (1 Cor. 12:18.)

_____

_____

_____

4. How are you to minister to your brethren? (1 Cor. 12:25.)

_____

_____

_____

5. What happens to the Church if *you* do not do your part?

_____

_____

_____

6. What makes the Body of Christ weak?

_____

_____

_____

Day Two

1. What was Moses anointed to do?

    _____

    _____

    _____

2. What did God do when the job became too big for Moses alone?

    _____

    _____

    _____

3. Whose anointing did the 70 receive?

    _____

    _____

    _____

4. What were they supernaturally empowered to do?

    _____

    _____

    _____

5. In addition to the anointing, what else did those 70 elders share with Moses?

    _____

    _____

    _____

6. What is your pastor sent by God to do in the Church?

   _____

   _____

   _____

7. What is *your* job in the Church? (Eph. 4:12.)

   _____

   _____

   _____

Day Three

1. Who did God give Moses to help him?

   _____

   _____

   _____

2. What does the word *minister* mean?

   _____

   _____

   _____

3. How is a person who serves his pastor like a waitress?

   _____

   _____

   _____

4. Why did God give Moses a man to serve him?

   _____

   _____

   _____

5. How will it help your pastor if you serve him as Joshua did Moses?

   _____

   _____

   _____

6. In Acts 6:2, what did the apostles say was their primary duty?

   _____

   _____

   _____

7. What benefits did Joshua derive from faithfully serving God's chosen man?

   _____

   _____

   _____

Day Four

1. How long did Elisha serve Elijah?

   _____

   _____

   _____

2. Why did the Lord have Elisha serve Elijah for so long?

_____

_____

_____

3. When does God promote someone?

_____

_____

_____

4. How do you prove your faithfulness to God and man?

_____

_____

_____

5. What did Elisha receive for his faithful service to Elijah ?

_____

_____

_____

Day Five

1. Who qualifies you for the ministry of helps?

_____

_____

_____

2. What important ingredient can only you bring to the ministry of helps?

_____

_____

_____

3. What belongs to the faithful? (Prov. 13:17.)

_____

_____

_____

4. What is another characteristic of a faithful servant? (Prov. 14:5.)

_____

_____

_____

5. What effect does the faithful servant have on the one he serves?

_____

_____

_____

6. What will you abound in if you are faithful? (Prov. 28:20)

_____

_____

_____

Chapter 10: Lesson Three

Day One

1. What does it mean to be "doubleminded" in your calling from God?

   _____

   _____

   _____

2. What does James 1:7 say the doubleminded person receives from God?

   _____

   _____

   _____

3. What are you to be for your pastor? Why has God put you in his church?

   _____

   _____

   _____

4. What does Proverbs 29:18 say about people without a vision?

   _____

   _____

   _____

5. What happens to those who act on the part of the pastor's vision which God has given them?

_____

_____

_____

6. How do you protect the vision God has given you? (Hab. 2:2,3.)

_____

_____

_____

7. Why should you write down what God has told you to do in the church?

_____

_____

_____

Day Two

1. What vision did God give Abraham that exercised his faith?

_____

_____

_____

2. What is another name for supernatural hope?

_____

_____

_____

3. What are the four kinds of visions God gives?

_____

_____

_____

4. Why would God give you the same vision as your pastor?

_____

_____

_____

5. What did Abraham have to do to receive the fulfillment of the vision God gave him?

_____

_____

_____

6. What causes people to fail? (Prov. 29:18.)

_____

_____

_____

7. What does faith bring to pass? (Heb. 11:1.)

_____

_____

_____

Day Three

1. What part did Moses' helpers play in the battle with Amalek?

   _____

   _____

   _____

2. Who did God tell how to win the battle?

   _____

   _____

   _____

3. When God gives a man a vision, what else does He give him to carry it out?

   _____

   _____

   _____

4. How does God reveal His will, or goal, for your church?

   _____

   _____

   _____

5. Why should you be careful not to criticize or run ahead of your pastor in God's work?

   _____

   _____

   _____

Day Four

1. In your own words, write down what it means to be knit together as one man.

    _____

    _____

    _____

2. On what does the success of the Church in this world depend?

    _____

    _____

    _____

3. What is the best way to beat an army?

    _____

    _____

    _____

4. What is Satan trying to do to God's army?

    _____

    _____

    _____

5. Who will God work with? (1 Cor. 3:9.)

    _____

    _____

    _____

6. Why must you work together with your brothers in the Lord?

_____

_____

_____

7. What elements are included in God's idea of unity? (1 Cor. 1:10.)

_____

_____

_____

Day Five

1. What aided the growth of the early Church?

_____

_____

_____

2. Who did God appoint to lay hands on the ministry of helps?

_____

_____

_____

3. Why did the Word of God increase?

_____

_____

_____

4. Why did Stephen get promoted to a miracle-working ministry?

_____

_____

_____

5. Why did God set the ministry of helps in the Church?

_____

_____

_____

6. How did God equip the seven men for the ministry of helps?

_____

_____

_____

Part Three:
Feedback

12

Introduction:
General Principles and Guidelines

In every seminar, there generally are some questions about principles and guidelines on choosing helpers and dealing with them. Following are some of the general guidelines I usually give pastors and church leaders.

Simply accepting everyone who wants to be an usher or door greeter is as dangerous as accepting someone who offers to sing in the choir — then finding out the person cannot carry a tune!

The atmosphere in your church will benefit from heading off possible areas of strife and confrontation before they come into being. So, how do you know which people really are called to a ministry of helps and, if so, where to put them?

At one church where I was involved, my job was to find a place for people who wanted to help. The first thing I did was try to find out their true motives and attitudes.

I had a plaque on my wall that read, *Be leery of those who seek authority but grab hold of those who want responsibility.*

So the first question I asked any volunteer was, "We are cleaning the church next Saturday. Can you be here for that?"

Some people only wanted to be teachers. They wanted authority. Another way of finding out people's motives was, for example, if they offered to usher, letting them read the guidelines for ushers. Sometimes that made them certain they wanted to usher; other times, it let them realize beforehand that they did not want to.

After you once set someone into a position, the only way out — if he or she does not work out — usually is strife. And strife may take them out of the church as well as out of the position. If they know in advance what is expected, it helps to weed out those who are not sincere.

Also, the church leadership needs to place value on what the helps ministries are doing. People will do what the church leadership does. If your pastor is not respected in the church, it is because the leadership does not respect him or her. Leaders are an example. If there is strife in the church, you can pretty much tell there is strife in the leadership.

Another bottom line is: When a person is anointed, he or she brings forth fruit, and the fruit will define the office or duty in the church. The fruit of the life will label the person. People bearing fruit will not need a pastor to label them.

Pastors, you must present the whole vision of the church and ministry to the people. And you must trust your workers. If you seek the Lord concerning His will for placing anyone in a position, and if you find out the motives and attitudes of those who offer to work, it will be a peaceful situation. You will not place people where they are not supposed to be or where they will not work.

I would strongly suggest writing out guidelines for each position, then people know what is expected of them and what is not. Otherwise, how will your workers know what you want them to do?

Knowledge eliminates fear. If anyone has fear, it is usually because of the unknown. Giving your people knowledge will eliminate many fears of "what if, what if?" Training also is really important. We took two years to train workers in one church where I was involved.

But remember, *Jesus is a shepherd, not a dictator.* Therefore, He will rule — and you should rule — out of the level of submission to you, *not by force.* The more you submit to Him, the more He will use you. But Jesus will not *force* you to serve Him. And you cannot *force* workers to serve. Be consistent and firm with your helpers and associates, but do not be overbearing. That is how to build trust. If they do not trust you, they will not be able to feel confident in what they are doing.

Answering the Call

Some of you readers may be thinking, "When I am equipped, I'll do what God wants me to do. I'm not ready now."

For God hath not given us the spirit of fear; but of power, and of love, and of a sound mind.

2 Timothy 1:7

These three things are the usual excuses pastors hear for people not wanting to move out on their callings: "I don't have the ability, I can't do it in love, and I'll go crazy (if it is dealing with children)!"

However, if God is calling you to do something, and you step out in faith, He will honor your obedience by giving you the love, ability, and lack of fear to do it. At first, you may be shaky and uncertain, but soon, it will seem as if you have always done this job. You will look back and wonder how you could have been fearful about it.

First of all, everyone in the helps ministry needs a close relationship with Jesus. You are in the church to serve God, and through His will, place, and timing, to serve your brothers and sisters in the Lord. But you are not there to please men.

Secondly, you need to keep looking at your ministry with a fresh eye. When I worked in a church at anything, about every three months, I would stop and look at what I was doing and why.

I would ask myself this question: "Who put me here? Did I put myself here, or did God?"

There have been many times when I would have to swallow hard and admit it was me, then go to those in charge and ask to be taken out of that position. That is not easy to do. The best way is to be sure ahead of time that God is placing you there.

Placing yourself in an area is where the turmoil starts and trouble begins. Sooner or later, you will leave that position, or be asked to, and that is usually where strife enters. If you are in the wrong area, admit you have made a mistake and peacefully move out. If where you are *is* a mistake, it was your idea. God does not make mistakes.

Once, as an usher, I had the responsibility of putting water on the platform. At one point, I felt I had grown beyond putting water on the platform, so I gave that job to another usher. Later, when I took a look at myself, I had to ask who had prompted me to give up the water detail — me or God? I had to admit it was me. So I had to go back to the other usher, apologize, and ask if I could again put water on the platform until I was relieved of that by the Holy Spirit or the head usher.

To maintain your spiritual walk, it is vital that you stop periodically and check yourself:

Did God put you where you are, or did you put yourself there?

Did God tell you to leave the place where you are, or did the flesh just get bored and want to do something new?

13

Questions and Answers on the Ministry of Helps

One question that I hear frequently is: "How do you distinguish between a call to a certain ministry and seeing a need that you have the ability to meet?" Another frequent question is: "How do you know what to do when you have the ability and are available to do a job, but you already are involved in something else?"

In either case, my advice is to just pick up the phone and volunteer to do whatever is needed. People use the phrase, "Well, I'm just not called in that area," to avoid helping out. You were called the day you got saved. When you were born again, you were adopted through the Lord Jesus Christ into the family of God. His family is no different than an earthly family in this respect: If the whole family prospers and loves one another, then every family member has to pitch in and help.

Suppose your mother said to you as a child, "I need the beds made or the dishes washed," or your dad said, "I need garbage carried out," or whatever.

Would you have told them, "I'm sorry, but I've not been called in that area?"

Of course not. Then why do we think we can put off our heavenly Father that way when He has chores that need doing?

I have never been "called" to this ministry. I just began to do the things God told me to do. I did not want to do all of them, but I do what He brings me to do. God does not move on behalf of status; He moves on behalf of His servants.

So many people want a "calling." As a Christian, you want to serve God. That is a calling in itself. If you move out and "do what your hand finds to do," God will begin to speak to your heart about the area where He wants to use you. A car has to be in gear and moving before you can turn it in a certain direction.

When I took a position on the staff of a large church some years back after having been in a traveling ministry for several years, some people told me I was moving backward. I was concerned about that, and one day as I was flying somewhere, I asked the Lord if I was moving backward.

He said, "Buddy, how much money are you budgeting for the six departments that you oversee right now?"

I said, "A million and a half dollars."

He said, "When was the last time you had to handle $1.5 million?"

I said, "Lord, I guess I'm moving forward, not backward!"

Door Greeters

Q. As a greeter, is it inappropriate to say, "Good morning, how are you?" I feel as if I am putting people on the spot. What is a better way to greet people?

A. What you are saying sounds fine to me. Jesus answered a lot of questions with questions. If you are too "gushy" or sound phony, nothing you say will give them a genuine sense of welcome. Just be "real," and greet people the way you would like to be greeted.

Q. How would you handle dress codes for greeters and ushers? And, when you set codes, what about those who think you are getting legalistic? Is there a good way to get your point across without sounding like, "If you don't like it, leave"?

A. One thing to begin with: If you are going to write guidelines, follow them, because once you compromise, you might as well throw them away. Some Christians who are young in the Lord will try to see how far they can go. In that case, you will just have to tell them, in love, that this is the way it is in your church. But communicate with them.

I am a firm believer that each department should have its own guidelines, because each department has different needs. If you make one dress code and guideline for the whole church, you have eliminated a lot of people from participating. For example, in the nursery, the babies and toddlers could care less if you have on a suit and tie, or a dress and hose. They just care if your hands are warm and your voice loving.

Years ago, I was pretty adamant about ushers wearing suits and ties. Then I was preaching in a church in Spokane, Washington, and a man from Idaho came up to me after the service.

He said, "Brother Bell, I understand what you are saying about ushers and dress, but I don't really think there is a tie in the whole town I come from."

I went home and prayed, and the Holy Spirit spoke this to me: "Use the pastor and his wife as a dress-code example. What they wear is what the ushers or greeters should wear, because they are before the people, also."

Once a man came to me and wanted so sincerely to be an usher, but he did not have a suit or tie. In this church, there were 35 ushers. If I had bent the rules for this one man, the next week, I would have had them all in my office wanting to know why they had to wear ties, and he did not.

So I said, "Why don't we find you a job in the church where you don't need a suit and tie, and we'll believe God for a suit and tie for you," and he agreed.

About two months later, one day after service, he came running up to me with something in his hand, and said, "Brother Bell, someone gave me a suit and tie today. Can I be an usher now?" He was one of the best ushers we ever had there.

When I did not bend the rules and let him usher according to his circumstances, that put value on being an usher. Often, we pastors and leaders do not put value on working in the church. We treat it as a "have-to," not a privilege.

Nursery Workers

Q. Suppose all your life, you have wondered what you are supposed to be doing. Then you get saved, and you are five years into your Christian walk, but you still do not know. However, all your life you have had this idea in the back of your mind that you want to work in the nursery. Yet you are not sure you like children or that you can communicate with them. Do you still wait to try your hand at the church nursery, feeling you are not yet ready? Or do you do it now, trusting God?

A. What is happening in your case are those three things we talked about earlier: fear, "I do not have the ability," and "I'll go crazy." Move out, and trust God to help you!

Q. You said earlier that a church should have one worker for every six children. What if you do not have that many workers?

A. Well, obviously, you must do with what you have. Pray for more helpers. And I would take only as many babies as you can effectively minister to and care for.

Q. Do you recommend that children's workers do extra activities outside the church? And do you recommend taking — say, 40 children — outside all at once?

A. That is a question for your pastor to decide. However, if I were a pastor, I would look at the limitations of the church, and at the transportation. Also, the responsibility involved and whether such practical things as insurance are in order.

When I worked in one large church, they had eight buses when I began to oversee the helps ministries — and only two of them ran. I proposed to clean them up. I called a bus company and had them pick up four of the buses and all of the other junky vehicles people had given the church. We began to believe God for good buses. When I left that church, there were five top-of-the-line buses that ran, and they were on a monthly maintenance program.

When a Christian school team went on an activity, they went on the #1 bus, and that did something for those kids. The buses were washed and cleaned out every week. The drivers were required to pass the city bus driver's test. So what you do with the children depends a lot on the equipment and trained personnel that you have.

Q. How can I get nursery workers together to pray before the service, and how can I meet with them without the distraction of the children?

A. Have your people come in a few minutes early and arrange for someone else to look after the children of the nursery workers for the few minutes necessary. Or, you might rotate your workers, having one each service watch the children while the others meet. Have the workers purpose to pray on the way to church.

Q. I know nursery workers are important in the natural, but are they important in the spiritual area?

A. I saw a mother get saved one time as a result of the nursery worker. The worker did not lead her to the Lord, but the mother had attended church and left her baby in the nursery. All that week, the baby had been so good that the next Sunday that mother asked the nursery worker what on earth she had done to the baby. The nursery worker told her it was just Jesus in her and His love that had been felt by the baby. The woman went into the service and got saved. So, if you have a responsibility, take care of it. Do not neglect it because it does not seem important. You may get to heaven before you find out all of the results of your faithful obedience in the nursery — or in other areas.

Q. You stress the importance of having good people working in the nursery. But some churches use teenaged girls. Do you think that is a good idea?

A. Usually, it is not hard to get teenaged girls to work in the nursery. Do you know why? Because they are on the threshold of adulthood, they may not be comfortable in the adult services. The pastor and the Word of God are pushing them to step through to adulthood, and it is easier to stay on the child side. So to do that, they will volunteer to work in the nursery without realizing why. If you do not have quality children's workers, begin to pray for God to send you some.

Q. Is it not important for the workers to also hear the messages? If a helps ministry, such as nursery or ushers, works every service, when do they get to hear the Word of God?

A. That is a very good point. If your workers do not get the Word of God in them to build faith, their works will die. Do not work them until they die spiritually. Do not work people until they do not come back to church, and then shrug it off as their problem. The problem was they had someone over them who did not care about them. First Corinthians 12:25 says:

> That there should be no schism in the body; but that
> the members should have the same care one for another.

Have your workers rotate: work one service and attend the next. I know that takes a lot of workers, but that is an ideal to work toward.

Parking

Q. How do you keep people from parking in spaces marked reserved for the handicapped?

A. Well, usually you feel like flattening their tires! But, of course, you cannot do that, not legally nor in Christian love. The key again is communication. However, it is amazing how many people drive onto church property and think the laws of the land no longer apply.

In an instance like this, I would just be standing near the car when that person came out of church. Then I would explain that, by parking there, they may have kept some handicapped person from hearing a Word of God from God that he or she needed that very day. If they do it again, you meet them again after the service. It will not take but a time or two, until they will begin to find another space.

Just remember not to "lose your cool." These situations many times are real tests on the fruit of the Spirit within you. Also, if you do not get rude or mean with the people, they cannot complain to the pastor about you.

Praise and Worship Leaders

Q. Are your singers and praise and worship leaders also in the helps ministry? And how should they operate with the pastor and with visiting speakers?

A. Yes, even the musicians are in the helps ministry. Hopefully, they set themselves to work under the pastor, not to do their own thing. The music and the rest of the service should flow together. This is a team operation, not a group of individuals following their own paths.

Concerning visiting speakers: The praise and worship leader should be willing to ask if the songs he or she has picked fit with the message. And it would be helpful if the pastor would find out from his guest how he (or she) likes the music to be, or how he (or she) feels the music should be during *this* service. Most ministry gifts would really appreciate this.

I have had music people put the congregation to sleep, and it might take me thirty minutes into my message or teaching to get them spiritually awake. Perhaps if the musicians had come to me, we could have worked together to get the people "up" in the spirit quickly and ready to receive from the Lord.

Some churches where I have spoken, I have "come out running," then after a few minutes, looked back, and they were all still at the starting gate. Then I had to backpedal and pick them up.

I have been in services where only the last song wakes people up. There is nothing wrong with a worship service, if that is the way the Holy Spirit is moving. My point is: Do not work against the speaker, whether he is quiet or excitable. A very helpful thing for pastors to do is ask the visiting speaker to pray for the workers before the service. That brings a unity between them.

Miscellaneous Subjects

Q. When you have an altar call, and perhaps 150 people come forward, how can you organize things without quenching the Holy Spirit?

A. The organization should come before the people come forward. Do not wait until you already have them standing around the altar before you figure out how to handle the ministry.

Meet with your ushers and counselors and arrange who is to be where and what each is to do before you have meetings where large numbers may end up at the altar or up front to be ministered to.

In addition, if you have a visiting speaker in your church, tell him or her ahead of time what room to send people to if there is an altar call. Visiting speakers will not know whether your ushers or counselors are prepared. If it looks as if there is no planned organization, they may hold back and that will quench the Spirit of God.

It is a good idea to write down on a file card your preparations for contingencies that might arise in a meeting and give it to a visiting speaker. Make a note of such things as that your praise and worship leader or pianist is very attuned to the Spirit and can flow with His moves, as well as whether you have another room to send people and whether you have trained counselors.

Q. Does "helps" go beyond working in the church?

A. Yes, rendering assistance or giving helps to the weak or the needy. I even believe anyone who is doing their day-to-day work is operating in the ministry of helps. God will help you on your job. You are a Christian at work as well as in church and at home. Some people try to fit church into their lives: "If I have time, I'll go to church." I do not think that way. Everything I do is centered around God and His work. Before I was in full-time ministry, I expected God to help me on my job.

I already was operating in the ministry of helps when I learned about it. The helps ministry goes beyond the four walls of the sanctuary. When you are prompted to render assistance or give help to the sick or needy, that is God working. A lot of people are moved by the Holy Spirit to do such things, but then they take the credit to themselves.

Q. What about the ministry of governments?

A. I believe the ministry of governments has not been fully tapped yet. Governments and helps are to work and flow together. Governments deals with leadership and should be emphasized in today's church just as much as helps.

Q. How do you deal with a supervisor who is trying to put onto you things that are his job or things he does not want to do?

A. About the only thing you can do is pray for hidden things to be brought to light (1 Cor. 4:5), pray for God to bring what is happening to the attention of someone in leadership. In the meantime, keep your attitude consistent with the fruit of the Spirit, and do the work as best you can.

If you become a supervisor, be certain to keep your attitude right. Sometimes we think we know better how to direct someone else's life than that person does. We need to pay attention to our shortcomings, not others' shortcomings: Am I where God wants me? Am I doing what God wants me to do?

I used to think, "Okay, God, You can sit down. I'll take care of this."

Then I found out that He wants to be involved in the Church. He wants to handle things. Just take care of yourself, and God will take care of your brother.

I was teaching along this line one day, and a woman came up to me and said, "Brother Bell, I'm kind of upset with you."

I said, "Oh, no! I thought everyone loved me."

She said, "See those two people sitting together back there? I have been working with them for months, and because of your little teaching today, I'm going to have to start all over again!"

I said, "Well, Ma'am, I'm sorry I interfered with your guinea pigs."

And that is exactly what those two people were to her. She was running their lives. It is time we let God back into the Church. It is time we let people hear from God. Clay cannot shape clay. Only the Potter shapes and molds us.

Q. How do you get people in the church to work?

A. Sometimes the only thing that motivates people is examples. Some people are working in churches today because of seeing me and my wife work and be committed.

Q. If they have an example, how do you keep them from copying the example? How do you get them to follow their own paths?

A. Pastors in general need to learn how to manage people. I can go into a lot of churches and motivate people to get behind the pastor. However, what happens when I leave many times is that the pastor does not know what to do with them.

I am not talking about manipulating people. I am talking about *leading* them, getting them into the Word of God, *expecting* them to do certain things. That is what motivates people.

Leaders should be saying, "I want you to be a success. I want you to fulfill everything God has for you," not, "You're *going* to be a success, do you hear me?"

Give people a positive goal to reach towards, not a negative one. For many years, leaders have presented the negative. You cannot fight the negative with the negative. You have to overcome evil with good. Teach them something positive. Fight the negative factor in their lives with the positive.

This subject came up in a pastor's conference in Florida early in the Eighties, and the Lord spoke forth in a prophecy:

There are those of you here, saith the Lord, who wonder how to inspire in your workers the loyalty and dedication you have seen demonstrated here. Here is the key. If you will submit yourself to Me, and discipline yourself to follow Me closely, showing unto me the same loyalty and commitment you desire your workers to show toward you, then I, the Lord, will inspire your workers to show that same loyalty and submission to you.

To the same extent that you submit yourself to Me, I will inspire them to submit to you. Do not try to force them or manipulate them into being submissive. If you will simply set your eyes on Me and follow Me closely, then without any conscious effort on your part, I, the Lord, will move upon men's hearts to follow you as you follow Me and serve you as you serve Me. It is that simple, saith the Lord.

Ushers

Q. One thing I find difficult is that often, when I ask people if I can take them to a seat, they say no. Then I watch them look all over the church and perhaps take five or more minutes to find a seat. What would be a good way to handle that situation?

A. A lot of times, roping off sections and opening them only as needed will solve that. Or, you could have an usher stand at a row until it is filled, then move to the next one. Some people just do not like to be escorted, and you will have some "sheep" jump the gate. Just do not lose your salvation over it! Ushers really have to be on their toes because they handle the public.

People who attend may not all be members. Some may not even be Christians. As an usher, your attitude should be kind and peaceable. If you are easily offended, you need to let God deal with that before you move into any kind of public position.

People who come to church have been at work all week, perhaps being yelled at by bosses, so that they are already touchy. Realize that, and be prepared.

Everyone you seat, or try to seat, is not going to be an angel. Your job is to minister to them through your attitude so they will be able to receive the Word of God.

Q. I would like to know how you handle chronic problems. For example, how *do* you handle people who sit in the roped-off areas or hold up the back wall? How do you deal with people who continually walk out of the service and spend a lot of time outside the auditorium against the obvious wishes of the congregation and the pastor?

A. I am a great believer in communication. I discovered through trial and error that if you will go and talk to that person, there may be a reason for their getting up and leaving. Perhaps it is medical. If so, try to arrange to give them a particular seat on the aisle in order that their moving in and out will not distract others. And explain to them about distraction. Tell them nicely and lovingly that one little distraction might cause someone to miss the one Word from God that He brought them there to receive that day. As far as those who sit in roped-off areas, you only have two alternatives: leave them alone or ask them nicely to move.

Q. You told once of an incident when you were assaulted while you were speaking. What could a good usher have done to keep that situation from getting as far as it did?

A. The ushers did not move quickly enough in this instance. Also, there were two women ushers at each side of where this happened, and they were really upset. I do not believe women ushers should be by themselves. Pair them with a man, instead, simply because of possibilities like this.

The minute this man got up and began to talk or move, if I had been working as an usher, I would have approached him and placed my hand upon his shoulder. Instead, the ushers held back, giving the man time to get to me and begin to hit and bite me — and even then, there was no one there to help. He should have been stopped and removed.

You may have, or be in, a small church right now, but your church will grow, and you will not know everyone. That is when the devil will begin to slip in troublemakers or begin to stir up demonic disturbances. They could be worse than simply creating a scene.

Pastors have been shot in services. One evangelist tells of a man coming into one of his services with a pistol, planning to shoot him. But in prayer beforehand, the Lord revealed this to the ushers. So they were able to recognize the man and remove him. One pastor told me his first experience like this was as a teenager when an ex-con came into church looking for his wife. He shot the pastor with a double-barreled shotgun, then found his wife and shot her. The pastor said no one moved to try to stop the guy. The congregation just sat there in shock and let it happen.

As an usher, if you get a check in your spirit about someone, keep an eye on him. Do not kick him out without obvious reason, but be sure he sits where you want him to sit. Put an usher right beside him.

14

Comments From
Ministry of Helps Seminars

• I am just seeing how disorganized I have been. I am the leader of the ministry of helps, which I did not realize until I came to this meeting. I am excited, and I am believing for the zeal of God to return to my life so I can impart it to those who are under me. I want to see the ministry of helps really come forth in our church.

• I, too, have been serving in helps and did not know it until now. I have come so alive and on fire to share this with everyone else in our church. I see them doing the same thing — serving, but not knowing that is what God has called them to do.

• I feel like a sponge, absorbing all of this revelation. I am so blessed that the Lord sent me here in order for me to take this back to my church. The main thing I want to share with them is that they are not just workers. This is a ministry. They are not just cleaning the church. The Lord knows what they are doing. The Lord sees their hearts.

• Sunday morning before I came to this seminar, I was in the front of the auditorium patching some cords for the sound system, and I was really "burning" inside. The pastor asked me what was wrong.

I said, "It just seems as if the people in the ministry of helps aren't doing their part."

He said, "Well, it comes off sounding as if you are mad at *me*, or something."

Now, I see that I was not even doing my job. So I am motivated to do my job right and be an example.

• One thing I have learned is that we all go through the same things. I had never known what I was supposed to do in the ministry, like many others here. I spent three years asking God what He wanted me to do. I did not know that stepping into helping is a ministry.

People miss God so badly sometimes. They look way out there at the horizon, and the ministry is right at their feet. They do not know they are already in the will of God, passing the bucket, changing diapers, cleaning the church. You are in the will of God if you put all you have into what you are doing.

Early in my Christian life, I received a prophecy that said I would go around the world spreading the Word of God. Now, I have learned that I can be just where God wants me in the ministry by doing what I can right where I am. When I do what He tells me to do, then He will promote me according to what He wants.

• I have learned that encouragement and motivation come from the inside, not the outside. I had gotten stale, and I now realize it was not on account of my surroundings. I can rely on God to motivate me and to encourage me.

The other thing that I can take back with me is that helps is not just one department, one area of the church. Helps is being willing to do whatever is needed at any time.

Rev. Buddy Bell is a successful Author, International Teacher, and President and Founder of the Ministry of Helps International, Inc. in Tulsa, Oklahoma. His focus is the much needed message of the "Ministry of Helps." His insights into this Bible ministry have enabled countless people to find and fulfill their place in the local church.

Rev. Bell has traveled to over 1,000 churches teaching and helping church staffs and congregations awake to the power and plan of the Holy Spirit for accomplishing the work of the ministry through every believer.

Rev. Bell has authored *The Ministry of Helps Handbook* revealing how to be totally effective serving in the Ministry of Helps. He has also produced "The Complete Local Church Usher Training System," "Development of Local Church Leadership Notebook," and 20 videos utilized by over 5,000 churches worldwide.

Rev. Bell's humor, zeal and anointing from God to present the Ministry of Helps, motivates people in a most delightful manner.

"Known Throughout The Nation For Anointed Teaching, Life-changing Truths, and Hilarious Humor"

To contact the author, write:
Ministry of Helps International
P. O. Box 27366 • Tulsa, OK 74149
(918) 245-5768
E-Mail: mohi@mohi.org

Additional copies of this book are available
from your local bookstore.

Harrison House
P. O. Box 35035 • Tulsa, OK 74153

Other Products by Rev. Buddy Bell

Videos (VHS Only)

The Local Church Leadership Series
Faithfulness — the Crowbar of God
God Uses Both Stars and Candles
Jesus and the Ministry of Helps
Fear Not: Leadership, Organization and Structure
Guidelines: Yes or No?
How To Motivate Volunteers
Straight Talk to Leadership

The Local Church Motivational Series
The Zeal of God
The Word Works
How To Close the Door on Strife and Jealousy
     in the Local Church
Staying on Track With God
How To Deal With Burnout
Journey of a Servant

The Local Church Helps Series
Understanding the Ministry of Helps
Finding Your Place in the Local Church
How To Relate to Your Pastor
Winning First Time Visitors

The Local Church Servant Series
Ushering, in the Local Church
The First Look — Host and Hostess
Why Minister to Children?

Manuals

The Complete Local Church Usher Training System
     — the most complete course for ushers available
     — 2-hour video and 70-page training manual

Development of Local Church Leadership
     — bring organization and efficiency to
        your local church
     — 8 audio cassette lessons and study
        notes on leadership

Development of Local Church Membership
     — Everything you will need to make ministers out of your members
     — 4 video messages, workbook, spiritual gift test, and more

Books

Ushering 101
Greeting 101

Foreign Language Videos

Journey of a Servant
Fear Not: Leadership, Organization, & Structure Part 1 & 2
God Uses Both Stars and Candles
Becoming a Servant of Fire
Available Languages: Arabic, Chinese, German, Indonesian, Russian,
                    Vietnamese, Spanish, Portuguese, Tagalog, Korean,
                    Ukrainian, and Romanian
Available Formats: NTSC, PAL, SECAM, M-PAL, N-PAL, MESECAM